Take this t

before you read this book!

How do you get guys <u>to do what you want</u>?

Question 1:

Tomorrow morning you are filling up your car at the gas station and realize that you have $20 to get through the day *(including the gas you are pumping right now)*. Crap! You need another $20 "right now." What will you honestly do?

    A) Call daddy. I know he's at work but . . .

    B) Turn off the pump!!

    C) I flirt with the cashier. It *could* work(?)

    D) I go home and pack a brown bag lunch.

    E) I call one of my guy "friends" and have him bring me $40 and a salad at lunch.

Question 2:

Later tomorrow, you are hanging out at a local coffeehouse with a guy "friend" and he introduces you to a guy he works with. He is handsome, charming, friendly, *single,* and talks to both of you for a few minutes before running off to an appointment. What do you do?

    A) I hope he asks for my number.

    B) I GIVE him my number. No sense taking chances. Decent guys are hard to meet.

    C) I ask him out on the spot. (Why not?)

    D) I try to impress him with my wit. (Why not?)

    E) *(other)* _____.

Also by
Dusty White:

The Easiest Way
to Learn the Tarot—EVER!!

Dusty's newest book teaches you how to quickly and easily master the ancient secrets of the Tarot using revolutionary methods never before taught outside of secret mystery schools. All you need is this book and a deck of Tarot cards *(and some practice)*. If you have ever wanted to learn how to ask your guides for clear answers, have fun telling the fortunes of your friends, or even thought of one day becoming a professional *reader, you must read this book!*

This book is a complete step-by-step guide filled with clear, easy to follow examples and illustrations, and addictively fun exercises specifically designed to get you learning to *hear what your cards are telling you* from the very first day you start playing with them. Unlike other instruction methods that make you reliant on a book to decipher the meanings of the cards, you will learn exactly how to know what each card *means to you* every time it comes up in a reading. Most important of all—complete assistance in learning the Tarot and additional help are available to you 24 hours a day, 7 days a week at ***www.AdvancedTarotSecrets.com***. Stop in and visit us!

Also watch for:

Aphrodite's Book of Secrets
(How to get everything you want in life—
without a lot of hassle.)

Coming in 2009
www.EnlightenedSisterhood.net

How to Get ANY MAN to do ANYTHING You Want

How to find the ones you REALLY want

How to GET them

How to get them to buy you stuff!!

Second Edition

By the soon to be kicked out of the "men's club"
for revealing all of this to women

~~Dusty White~~

Illustrated by Katrina Joyner

Edited by Brenda Judy

BOOKSURGE PUBLISHING
North Charleston, SC

Printed by BookSurge Publishing, North Charleston, South Carolina

© 2006, 2008 by Dusty White First published 2007. Second edition published 2008
Illustration and image copyright © 2008 by Dusty White

Printed in the United States of America

All rights reserved. No part of this book may be reproduced or transmitted in any form or by any means, electronic or mechanical, including photocopying, recording, or by any information storage and retrieval system, without prior written permission from the publisher or the author. Contact the publisher for information on foreign rights.

Please note, this book is provided STRICTLY for entertainment purposes only. It is not designed to replace advice from a competent therapist. While it is hoped that you will enjoy this book, any advice contained here should be taken as a purely humorous look at the social interaction between women and men. Mention of specific brands, companies, organizations, or authorities in this book does not imply endorsement by the publisher, nor does mention of specific brands, companies, organizations, or authorities imply that they endorse this book. Internet addresses and telephone numbers given in this book were accurate at the time of publication.

ISBN 1-4196-6624-X

Library of Congress Cataloging-in-Publication Data

Library of Congress Control Number: 2008908611

About the cover model: Lidia Bergano (on the cover) is an environmental engineer by trade, and an artist by heart. Besides acting, modeling, and being a commercial film editor, she also participates in several projects for the artist community (www.starbuster.net). She lives in Portugal.

Clip-art thermometers on page 70 are from iCLIPART and are reproduced by permission. www.iclipart.com

Book design by House of White

To order additional copies, or for information on special discounts for bulk purchases, please contact BookSurge Publishing: 1-866-308-6235 or www.booksurge.com. Distributed to the book trade by Baker & Taylor, Inc. 1-800-775-1800 or www.btol.com

⊗ The paper used in this publication meets the minimum requirements of the American National Standard for Information sciences - Permanence of Paper for Printed Library Materials, ANSI Z39.48-1992.

This book is dedicated to
Vanese McNeill:

Wherever you are,
you make the sun shine brighter
for being there.

and to Kate Vavra,
Santa Cruz 1994

Contents

First ~~things~~ *lies* first

Screw *you!* I need to get MY needs met!

How guys learn about girls

Section 1
Guys: How to find the ones
you REALLY want

Section 2
Guys: How to meet them

Section 3
Guys: How to get them to do what you want

Section 4
Guys: Other Important Stuff

Appendices

Acknowledgements

A book this manipulative should never be written. Therefore, it is quite necessary to personally thank (in each and every copy) the wonderful women of Project Aquarius, without whose insistence I would have never embarked on this most diabolical of ventures.

As they are collectively the crème de la crème of some of the world's most gifted professional psychics, they know how much I love and appreciate them, every day, even after all of these years.

"All's fair in love and war"

– *Francis Edward Smedley*

"Kings will kneel before you,
for you are the source of their power"

– *Empoeirado Branco*

Introduction

I want you to be able to know where you stand with any man before you say "yes" and what will happen after you do. By knowing how your man thinks *before you get involved with him,* you transcend the war of the sexes and start dating intelligently. This will put *you* back in control and make all of your subsequent interactions with men <u>infinitely easier</u>.

~~LIES~~
First ~~things~~ first

I want to acquaint you with some commonly held beliefs among women: beliefs I have heard (and read) over the years, *many of which have been created and propogated by men.* You may already know some of these:

"Men rule the world"

"It's a man's world"

"Men have (like) soooo many advantages"

"Men stack the odds in their favor"

"Blah, blah, blah . . ."

and so on . . .

LIES! All of them!

Men (most, individually; and all, collectively) have <u>one goal in life</u>:

Get women to worship us
the way we idolize/idealize women!

Get that through your head once and for all and you "win." Equality of the sexes has always been a disjointed dance, with someone always stepping on someone else's toes while trying to maneuver for a better position. Women think guys have it easy. Guys think women have it easy (because guys are biologically wired to drool at a passing hottie, just like Pavlov's well-trained canines). In fact, as "men" (I use the term loosely here), we know all too well that if we fail to act, there is a never-ending supply of men <u>who</u> <u>will</u>. If we "miss our chance," some other guy will jump in before we get a chance to rethink our desires.

Again: Most men see women as having a biological advantage when it comes to dating. THAT is why we spend money on you (to impress you). <u>In a man's mind</u>, a reasonably attractive girl can get just about any guy she meets if she knows what to say, how to present herself, and even unattractive girls* can get attention and affection any night of the week.

* "Unattractive" is <u>purely a subjective opinion</u> that applies to one, and only one guy (e.g., the one who is deciding what HE likes).

"We" think that "we" want you more than you want us. This creates a paradigm *where the average guy thinks that the average girl has an edge over him*. This is, in turn, reinforced by the vast number of horny men (single, married—pretty much any man with a pulse and access to a bottle of Viagra) who actively pursues "any woman who will have sex with him."

Sex has become the standard of ascertaining if a particular woman has any real interest in us. The problem with this is that sex does not always equate "commitment," so it gets confusing to everyone.

Sexuality, *especially feminine sexuality,* **has been both prized and repressed for so long** that for generations we now see it as a privilege (like driving). As a man, you are not allowed to have sex until a certain age—and even then, most guys have trouble finding or getting any. Of course, you must learn how to get women/girls *interested in you,* but sadly they do not teach that in school. The end result is that you usually get a bunch of guys acting stupid, hoping that will impress the women we meet.

With these kinds of beliefs feeding our opinions of the world around us, there will never be any true equality among the sexes. The whole thing is a complete mess. Whoever designed this screwball system of dating should be hauled out and publicly flogged. Instead of getting together and hammering out some form of compromise, so that we can all be happy, we end up collectively fighting each other for any edge we can get *so that we can get "our needs" met.*

Screw you!
I need to get <u>MY</u> needs met!

Competition is the art of tripping up your opponent while getting as far as you can, without losing a step in the process. Our system of dating is so saturated in competition that, as a result, it is so completely screwed up that the whole of it should be tossed (baby AND bath water), and new systems should be taught in school so that future generations might actually find some happiness and "World Peace."

This utopian ideal is entirely possible, but as this is not a book on philosophy, I will save the rants and instructions of revamping dating systems to create global harmony for another time. Right now, <u>all that matters is</u> that YOU get a date with a cute guy by Friday night, get your boyfriend to remember you are standing next to him when a pretty girl walks by, or your husband to lift (and then lower) the seat on a regular basis. As we live in an increasingly selfish society, your job (getting men to do *what you want*) becomes easier everyday—as long as you know the basic rules of influence and how to use them to reach your goals.

<u>Life is shorter than you think</u>: Don't wait for "someday" to get men to help make your life easier. Guys waste money on women every day. Why let them waste their money on harpies *when they can invest in <u>your happiness</u>?*

Allow me to share with you a vastly overlooked secret; one that will help you hold sway over even the most vehement womanizer's you will meet:

The more a man idealizes women (yes, this includes "s-e-x"), the more he needs from a woman to be complete, validated . . .

 . . . to feel "equal."

"Equal?!!"

Why do you think we have been hogging all of the best jobs for ourselves throughout the centuries?

As long as YOU get to decide whether WE are going to get any sex or _affection_ from you, we are going to grab every coin we can—so we can tease you with money, impress you with money, and if that doesn't work . . . well . . . *we'll just have to starve you out!* We'll keep all of the money for ourselves—that is until one of our buddies starts spending money on women (which will take about 5 minutes) and then the whole process starts all over again.

You see—guys just <u>don't feel complete</u> without a woman (*or many women*) to idolize them. Most guys are tired of *chasing* women. Of course, we still do, every chance we get, but <u>the very reason we become</u> rock/rap/country/gospel stars, celebrity athletes, zillionaires is because **we really want YOU to throw yourselves at US!**

No . . . <u>really</u>. This is what is going on in your boyfriend's head <u>right now</u>.

Having *you* chase after *us* for a change makes us feel "equal." We build great monuments, empires, even go to war; all to feed that subtle, but all-consuming need to find parity with you. This is why we beat other men DOWN, humiliate them, and castrate them.

By making ourselves feel superior to other men (at least as far as YOU are concerned) *and then destroying your self-confidence,* **it simply becomes a "logical" choice** that you would be irresistibly drawn to us. And "everyone knows logic always wins out."*

Yes . . . *men need women* for far more reasons than we will ever admit. We need a woman because we want to be more than the sum total of our accomplishments. We want to actually enjoy life; we want "the right woman," and since you can be "Miss Right" to so many men simply by being genuinely nice, friendly, graceful, a bit erotic, feminine, intelligent, supportive, and somewhat pretty, why not take advantage of that? Why not spread your influence all over? Why not let men do *your* bidding for a change?

---

* *"everyone knows logic always wins out."* One of the great misconceptions of time, yet also one of the most persistently held beliefs among men throughout history. Emotion under-cuts, guides, and biases logic beneath the conscious mind's ability to recognize that it is being manipulated by personal prejudices. Beware of "logic." Ultimately it is simply another pawn being manipulated by unseen hands to bludgeon other minds into acquiescence.

How guys learn about girls

There is no class in high school or college that teaches guys how to talk to, or interact with, girls. As for "dads teaching their sons," most of them are worthless. What we learn is what we pick up from other guys, mostly in the locker room.

We don't sit down like some damned therapy group and discuss our feelings. We hide our insecurities and complete lack of understanding of women, and act as if we know what we are doing so that we don't look weak. We are told "women *love* guys with confidence," so that's what we show you. This is also why we never, <u>ever</u>, ask for directions in front of you. Here is a glimpse into the secret school of "how to get chicks" we (as guys) all learn from:

Tony (local "stud")**:** The way to get girls to want you is to treat them like crap.

Joe (average guy, trying to figure out how to get a date)**:** It is?

Bob: Yeah, the *worse* you treat them the more they *want* you. Nice guys just get played. Bitches like *real men!*

Fred: Yeah. I tried being nice to girls I liked, but they all just wanted to "be friends." No dates for me at all. Screw that!

Joe: So, if I want that girl in 3rd period, I should treat her like crap?

Tony: No, dimwit. You have to impress her first. Get her to notice you without her knowing that you are trying to get her attention. <u>Make</u> her notice you, and then when you approach her, she already knows who you are. When you talk to her, *act like she is not worth your time,* like you have more important things to do than hang out talking. Make her think you are important. Chicks want guys who are popular or important . . .

. . . and so on. The words change, **but the lessons are always the same:** *"Nice guys are suckers who deserve to get used. If you want to get attention from women, <u>you have to be a jerk.</u>"*

This is not a book about rewarding bad behavior. This is a book on how to influence *the behavior you want from men.* The techniques you will find here are used by women on men, and by girls on boys, every day, everywhere, all over the world. They are being used right now, as you read this.

. . . and they work.

All over the world, *countless men did unbelievably stupid things <u>today,</u>* because their logic told them that by doing these incredibly stupid acts, girls they like would find them more attractive. Tomorrow, more men will do more ridiculous things—just to get women to "want" them. Men will steal, lie, cheat, beg, wage war, spend money, change what god they believe in, *and even wake up and drag themselves to work one-more-day at a job that eats away their very soul,* because there is a woman in their life that they cannot live without.

They may be married to her, dating her, or they may see her every day, but they haven't asked her out yet. <u>Every day</u>, millions of men, all over the world, do millions of things to please a woman they desire for one reason: When the woman accepts them, they feel better than they have ever felt in their life.

Now that's power. And you have it at your disposal. The choice is yours really. Use your femininity to get men to do what you want (and we will all be happy), or complain that men "do things" that upset you, and we will continue to guess what you want.

Section 1

Guys:

How to find the ones
you REALLY want

"So who is this 'Mr. Right,' why is HE so special, and where is he anyway?"

The idea of "Mr. Right" has been passed down over the generations *that for every woman there is the perfect man for her.* I laugh at the whole notion **and you should too.** Here's why: The concept of a perfect match, one that requires <u>no efforts</u> on your part, creates unreasonable expectations that force a disparity between "ideal" and "reality" that always leads to disappointment.

The truth of the matter is that there are a lot of available men (and more than enough who are not "available," but will still try) of varying quality, that you can choose from, but the odds are that you will generally meet the worst of them. The reason is that men who have something going for them in their lives, men who passionately live life with a purpose, are usually too busy living their dreams to hang out *"trolling for chicks."*

When you compare the promise of some mythological prince riding in on a white horse <u>to the reality women face every day</u> when it comes to dating, the thought of "settling" for less (of a man) than what you really want is a bit depressing. Personally, I suggest you start drinking heavily.

There may be ten thousand "perfect men for you" out there, in a sea of two billion men globally. Getting one to find you without handing him a guide dog and a map is only slightly easier than winning the lottery. Good luck getting one to knock on your door.

A much easier way to find guys you like is to cast your (seductive) nets wide, and drag the men to you like schools of fish. Then pick from the very best. This book will help you do EXACTLY that. If you find your prince along the way, Section 3 will help you keep him keeping you happy; after all, what good is a prince if he turns into the prince of couch potatoes?

It's time to stop waiting around for "Mr. Right" and start getting the men in your life to do right by you. Choose from the best, but remember to bring your tool kit. Even the best will need some repairs. (That part is up to you.)

Forget diamonds!
Why a little impatience
is a girl's best friend.

Okay, so you have this dream of finding the prince of your dreams: he's handsome, rich, rides a motorcycle, and starts fights in bars . . . blah, blah, blah. <u>Everyone has their own preferences</u>. Let's see how much time you have to spend with "Mr. Where-the-hell-is-he-anyway?"

Assuming you live to the ripe old age of 97 (which seems like a ripe old age to live to—you may live longer, but that is not the point), you will want to snag a decent guy in time to have your diamond wedding anniversary (whatever that is).

So . . . counting backwards, we have 28 years to get the kids out of the house (2.5 kids spread out an average of 3 years or so), 3–5 years of traveling the world and sharing endless "romantic moments" together, a short engagement (another year), a whirlwind romance (2 years of "dating"), and we are up around 34–35 years already gone. You will probably want to meet this amazing guy before you are 40, so that knocks off a few years.

But wait! *There's more!!* <u>Don't forget all of the jerks you have to date</u> while you are looking for that guy who is "just right for you."

All in all, that leaves you about 8–10 years to find "Mr. Right," no matter how old (or young) you are right now. Now that may sound like a long time, but remember that you have school, a job, or kids eating away 6–10 hours a day of your time, not to mention every one of your friends who are always whining at you to "spend time with them" (like you don't see them enough in pictures). Well, that eats up another 2–3 hours each day. And then there's sleep, eating, showering, and going to pee.

Finally, *subtract every 5–10 minutes of your day wasted* each time some creepy guy tries to hit on you. At this rate, you might as well hire a professional matchmaker to track down "Mr. Too-good-to-show-up-at-your-door-with-a-diamond-already."

Okay, so if you added up all of your free time (after skipping a few of your favorite TV shows to save time, and chasing away those pesky keep-you-from-finding-a-decent-guy "friends" of yours), *you still have about 37 minutes* over your lifetime to find the guy who will make all others seem boring and insignificant. With so little time, how will your prince ever find you? He won't. He's too busy arguing that he doesn't need a map, or to stop and ask for directions, because he is <u>confident</u> that at any moment he will recognize a landmark and everything will be okay.

So it's time to roll up your sleeves, because you are going to have to go find him. But no one ever said that finding true, absolute, and everlasting happiness was going to be easy. Just look around: With the divorce rate as high as it is, and the number of people cheating on each other who are NOT divorced, *it doesn't look like the current method* of "waiting for a decent guy to find you" *is working all that well for everyone else.*

It's time to make a plan. Don't worry, you will like this plan a lot, because it is easy and it is fun. We are going shopping—for a man, or if you prefer, many men. All that matters is that this will be the most fun you ever have shopping—I promise. Oh, and this shopping excursion won't cost you a dime. In fact, if you apply what you learn in this book, you should end up "being paid to shop," like a mystery shopper. After all, when shopping for guys, <u>don't you want to know</u> who is going to be generous with their time (and money) *before you get too serious about them?*

Just in case you don't know, a mystery shopper is hired by various retail stores to go buy things, and then report back to the companies on how well their employees treated the mystery shopper. Of course, the mystery shopper is reimbursed for all of her purchases. As far as jobs go, it doesn't sound too bad.

Now, the first rule of smart shopping is to know what you want before you leave the house. Sure, you can always see something in the window while you are out, but the more you know what you want, the happier you will be with your purchases once you get them home. What follows is a remarkably effective method I have used to help tens of thousands of clients *find exactly what they wanted* in life. It will help you weed through all of the poseurs and pretenders and get the man (or men) you want, leaving the idiots for someone else to spend playtime with. This *amazing method* is simply called:

The List

. . . and it always works. It is incredibly easy to use. Simply fill in the blanks. Once you have completed your list, we will go over how to use it to get exactly what you want in life now, instead of later.

These are the <u>ten</u> <u>most</u> <u>important</u> <u>things</u> I want MY man to be:

1: _____

2: _____

3: _____

4: _____

5: _____

6: _____

7: _____

8: _____

9: _____

10: _____

Ideas: (Use these or choose your own!)

<u>Financial condition:</u> Rich, reasonably well off, "can afford me," can afford rent, can afford coffee, okay I'll buy the coffee, I really don't mind a starving musician/*author*.

<u>Looks:</u> Handsome, cute—but not "too cute" for me, decent looking is okay, has his own hair, has most of his own hair, has any of his own hair, "you know . . . looks are really overrated," okay so he lives under a bridge and scares small children and goats.

<u>Personality:</u> He's really the nicest guy, he would make a good diplomat, he would make a good salesman, he gets along with his friends, he doesn't really like strangers, okay—so he's an ass; what of it?

And here are a few more things I would like, but are not *"must have's"*:

1: _____

2: _____

3: _____

4: _____

5: _____

The idea behind this is to <u>focus on what is really important to you</u>. When we meet people who have an impact on us, we tend to be "flash-blinded," as if we met them in a dark alley and they shined a bright light in our face. All we can see is that stupid light. *All other details tend to fade into the background.* We become obsessed with what is being shined at us, literally blocking every other detail out of our field of view. *We can't see their baggage.* This is what is meant by the phrase "love is blind."

Let's say your ex-boyfriend had a great smile, witty pick-up lines, he made you laugh, and other than that, he was a complete ass. What you saw in the beginning was just that stupid grin that made you think, "Wow, this guy is really great! He is intelligent, funny, cute" (and so on). In this example, you were "flash-blinded" because he kept dazzling you with a handful of his strong points.

This happens to everyone, almost every time we become infatuated with someone. We see one or a few qualities and we become so wrapped up in those that *we end up missing the signals* that there are some parts of their personality that we can't stand. By the time we start to notice their flaws, we are already in a state of feeling good about them, and <u>whenever we feel good about someone, we want to give them the benefit of the doubt</u>. We forgive, ignore, and even make excuses for their flaws. This is human nature; and it is a very good thing, except when we base our relationships on it. There are many variations of the story of a foolish man who makes a wish in front of an evil genie. He wishes for a mountain of gold, so the genie drops a mountain of gold on him.

This is how most guys date:

They say to themselves, *"I want a hot chick."* But do they ask for a girl <u>they can get along with</u>, someone who is loyal, *who actually likes them?* Do they ask for a woman who fits their secret ideal? Of course not! Don't be absurd! Most men are complete idiots when it comes to dating.

That is why it is so hard to tell the difference between the good ones and the losers who do their best to impress you for the first few days, weeks, or months (or hours in some cases). <u>Don't make</u>

9

<u>the same mistake</u>. *You* can get just about any guy to do anything with the right approach. But if you want to have a lot of fun (and make your life infinitely easier), pick the guys you can stand long enough to work with, instead of choosing guys who have (at best) only one or two qualities that you like.

The world's best chocolate
starts with the world's best ingredients

Words to live by. Now, with that out of the way, it is time to find out what you DON'T want. After all, what good is an Adonis if he comes with a whole shopping cart full of baggage?

Presenting:

The ~~other~~ List

At least 5 things <u>I refuse to accept</u>:

1: _____

2: _____

3: _____

4: _____

5: _____

(6?) : _____

(7?) : _____

Oh yeah! Here are some other things I don't like either:

1: _____

2: _____

3: _____

4: _____

Using the list is so easy you won't believe it can actually work. Grab a blank sheet of paper and fill in the things you want—and don't want. Your list is entirely personal, and you do NOT have to show it to anyone—especially NOT the guys you are rating. Remember that **you can change your lists** at any time. These lists reflect what is most important to you at this stage of life.

Once you have completed your lists, crossed out what you wrote and re-filled it in a few times, and you are finally happy with them, make a few photocopies of your lists, and on each copy write the name of a guy you like at the top. *Use that copy as a checklist* of how he rates on your personal scale. This will help you weigh *any man's* strong points versus his weak or average ones to see what it is about him that you love so much—and what it is about him you will eventually hate; but you get to see all of this well ahead of time. When you find areas of his personality (on your list/s) that you can't put down a solid answer, see that as a red flag that you need more information about this guy before you allow yourself to develop serious feelings for him. As rudimentary as this sounds, it <u>will</u> save you endless amounts of time, effort, frustation, **and sanity** later.

You are <u>making sure</u> that you are not flash-blinded *("but he's so hot/rich/nice," whatever)* by one or two qualities and missing clues on how you will be ignored or mistreated later. MOST PROBLEMS women face in life **are caused directly by** their choices in men. Your friends often can spot guys who are bad for you, even when you refuse to listen. Think of these lists as your best friends. They will never lie to you or let you date a guy who does not live up to your exact standards. These simple "shopping lists" will instantly weed out all of the jerks and idiots you think you like, before you actually develop any real emotional connection with them. They will save you time, money, and sanity.

Secrets from the Mystery School 101: The popular "law of attraction" is only one HALF of the "Laws of Attraction and Repulsion" equation. If you <u>fail</u> to specify what you do NOT want, you open yourself up for anything that even remotely resembles what you DO desire. <u>This is why</u> you have positive (attraction) and negative (repulsion) lists. For more secrets, visit us at **www.EnlightenedSisterhood.net.**

How this fits in with "impatience being your friend" and all that . . .

As kids we are all taught that "impatience is bad," and how we should always be patient (kind, polite, and a million other things we never seem to end up doing once we are adults). I have a different take on this whole impatience thing, and you will too after you read this next part.

Impatience is an amazingly wonderful trait when you carefully channel it. Impatience causes stress that makes you get off your butt and *go get what you want now*, rather than waiting around for someone to come along and hand it to you. **Politeness always counts**, of course, but the secret to enlightenment (and perpetual happiness) is to master the correct delivery of impatience and politeness. You can trust me on this, as in Tibet I am referred to as *his high holiness, the grand enlightened, wise, and compassionate swami who steps gingerly on lotus petals, drinks only caffeinated beverages, and whose long, broad tongue speaks only truth.*

A little impatience (carefully applied and infused with sincere politeness) will get more done, quickly and easily, than any amount of nagging, begging, or complaining *will ever get done.*

<u>Impatience is your friend</u> because it is always working for you, and *your needs*. Impatience will not let you waste your time dating a guy who refuses to give you the same affection and attention you lavish upon him. You will also not stay in a dead-end job for very long, missing out on the finer things in life.

While you are waiting for *"Mr. Can't-come-sweep-you-off-of-your-feet-because-he-is-too-busy-chasing-other-women"* to come sweep you off of your feet, <u>you are being assaulted</u> by wannabe "pimps," players, and all sorts of guys you have absolutely no interest in.

Life is happening *and you are NOT in that dream relationship,* traveling the seven continents without a care in the world, not to mention the fact that you are getting older every day.

Impatience can save you
from all of that!

Just click your heels together three times and say, "Impatience—take me away!" (or the ever popular "Screw this! I'm getting what I want!"), and then decide, once and for all, that this is *your* life and *you deserve* <u>whatever it is that you want from life</u> (until you decide you want something else instead), **and then go get it.**

Let other girls sit on their butts wishing for a perfect life. You have men everywhere who will cater to your every need—once you start asking them to.

Isn't that great?

Think of impatience as a little dog. As long as you keep your impatience on a leash, and clean up after it, you will have a faithful companion—one who is always happy to see you, and eager to go outside and play. Some people keep their impatience locked away inside until one day the pressure of *never satisfying their needs* makes them **snap.**

Don't be like that! Take your impatience out for walks daily. Make it a point to be selfish, <u>and spend some time every day thinking about what you want</u> from life. Look at your lists d-a-i-l-y. Dream of places you want to see, and decide when you want to see them.

At first this will seem a little absurd, because you may not be able to see at the moment *exactly how* you will get to see, do, or have all of these things in life. Stay at it. Every day make sure that you spend at least 5 minutes (twice a day—just like brushing) dreaming of what you want from life. An easy way to do this is to dream up what you want your life to be over a cup of coffee or tea.

Once you start doing this on a regular basis, impatience will kick in naturally, and you will begin to realize consciously *that you really do want more from life after all.* You will be surprised at the ways life bends to your will once you decide what you want, and how opportunities open up for you almost magically. Once you get in the habit of this, it will become extremely easy to influence people based on your desire to get things done "now," instead of when someone else thinks that it is convenient. Perfect your ability to phrase your *requests* in ways that make other people feel that this will be exciting and fun for them (as well as you) and that everyone will benefit. This keeps other people from thinking of you as a selfish bitch that always has to have her own way.

Assuming that you are going to be doing this from now on, *we now get to the fun part:* <u>Getting the most out of the men you date,</u> with as little hassle as possible. Please remember to come back and read all of the above again. Use a highlighter to mark the points you need to work on the most. Right now, I am going to show you how to use your impatience to get what you want from life, from men, *now*.

Let me introduce you to another little trick I have used to help thousands of clients find happiness in their lives. Below is a familiar picture. It is from the back of a one dollar bill (U.S.). If you need one to look at to compare with the image in the book, just grab a passing guy and ask him for a dollar.

The founding fathers were absolute geniuses of symbolism. Much has been said about the "eye and the pyramid," mostly by conspiracy nuts. **I will now reveal to you the real secrets of this ancient symbolism,** and how they affect your everyday life:

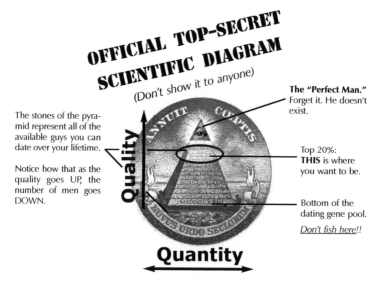

OFFICIAL TOP-SECRET SCIENTIFIC DIAGRAM
(Don't show it to anyone)

The stones of the pyramid represent all of the available guys you can date over your lifetime.

Notice how that as the quality goes UP, the number of men goes DOWN.

Quality

The "Perfect Man."
Forget it. He doesn't exist.

Top 20%:
THIS is where you want to be.

Bottom of the dating gene pool.
<u>*Don't fish here!!*</u>

Quantity

This is a picture of all of the guys you will EVER date and a whole lot that you will never get to meet. The row of stones at the very bottom of the pyramid (*the row with the letters MCQXXLZ . . .*) represents every guy alive right now. If you say to yourself, *"I want a man!"*, here's were you will find them all. That bottom row of stones represents an unfiltered pool of fish to choose from. You reach in your hand and pull out a fish. Will it be a shark? A piranha? A salmon? Who can say?

But no one dates at the bottom of the gene pool. We all have some qualification(s) we quietly put on our future spouse. Each time you start putting qualifications on what you will accept in the men you date (see your list(s) from above), you are in effect "raising your standards."

This takes you another step up the pyramid.

If you say, "I will not date men who are emotionally unavailable," then you jump up a few levels of stones on the pyramid. <u>You have fewer men to choose from</u>, but the quality of the men you *do* date is much better.

This all should sound elementary. You should *know this*. The sad fact is, however, that <u>every day women continue to fail to apply these basic rules of dating</u>. **As a result, they are very unhappy.** We all make exceptions for people, fall in love with one or two aspects of someone, and ignore the parts we do not like until we simply cannot stand it any more. This is a recipe for disaster—and it is a perfect recipe. It never fails to produce disaster.

Fortunately, you already possess the tools you need to avoid the pitfalls everyone else makes in relationships, and start getting what you want from life. But before we solve this problem, I want you to know a little more about the ancient symbolism and how looking at a dollar bill from now on will remind you of the importance of having personal standards.

That glowy part around the eye atop the pyramid is the amount of love you have to extend to bridge the gap between your "ideal" and the guy you end up settling for. The best you can hope to find is a guy at the very top of the pyramid. Notice how even this amazing man does not quite reach your ideal (the floating eye). Can you see how the glowy part only extends to the first few levels of stones? That is no accident. The glow is a visual representation of the amount of (reasonably unconditional) love you can comfortably offer over extended periods of time.

You can easily glow to the top of the pyramid. Anyone can love someone who is genuinely nice, friendly, attentive, beautiful, strong, intelligent (and so on . . .). The real challenge is extending that untiring love down a few levels. The more you have to "glow," the more stressful the relationship becomes.

If you are dating a guy who matches your needs moderately (about halfway up the pyramid), you have to continually stretch the amount of love, patience, compassion, communication, affection, trust (and so on), to keep this relationship alive and happy. That gets really old—really fast. Before you know it, you are a walking stress ball, wondering why you put up with all of it.

Just to make sure that we are perfectly clear, because the rules of relationships do not change:

The problem is that most women <u>end up meeting guys that far exceed the quality of the ones they settled for</u>. Don't make their mistake. *You are worth more*. Your new mantra should be:

"No more frogs!"

So . . . now that we have an understanding of what is out there and why the guys you meet treat you the way they do, it's time for . . .

Rule #3:

(Okay . . . so "Rule #1" actually appears a bit later in this book—but— if you read the book backwards, Rule #1 would actually come first.)

*D*ecide <u>what kind of guy you want</u>!

It's just like buying shoes . . .

Brainy?

. . . sometimes you just have to try on a few to see how they fit your lifestyle.

Chatty . . .

What you think you may have wanted yesterday . . .

"No, really honey. Just let me get 3 more levels in Wizard Fire for my elf shamman on World of Warcraft and THEN we can go see a movie!"

. . . may be boring to you today.

"Hot misunderstood tattoo artist-guitarist-in-a-band guy you met at a party last Saturday"

Who can say, when it comes to affairs of the heart?

Bad boys are sexy.

Danger, action . . .

. . . or was it romance
you were looking for?

Which one is right for you?
(at the moment)

"I don't like men with <u>too many</u> muscles"
- Janet (*Rocky Horror Picture Show*)

Section 2

Guys:

How to meet them

(the ones _you really want,_
not just "any guy")

In a guy's mind . . .

<u>How the average guy works a party, the bar</u> . . .

☞ Arrive; do a quick scan for "hot girls." Do nothing about it.

☞ Look for friends—or anyone familiar enough to say hello to. Hopefully someone (or enough people) will "know you" to welcome you and show you (or at least tell you about) the best parts of the party: the bar, the pool, "party room," or at least where the "hottest girls" are hiding out.

☞ Get a drink or two (also known as "liquid courage"—*for good reason*).

☞ Talk to friends (if any can be found).

☞ If no friends around, look for something to do. Think about "hot girls" he saw earlier.

☞ If that fails, look around the place for someone easy to talk to—maybe they know some "hot girls."

☞ Think about some girl who is talking to someone else.

☞ *Drink more.*

☞ *(optional)* Get frustrated that "hot girl" didn't come on to him; make an ass of himself.

☞ Look for any girl to talk to.

☞ Hope to go home with (or at least get the phone number of) *any girl*.

☞ Wake up with a mild hangover.

There are, of course, any number of minor variations on this theme, but the process is fairly universal. Every guy's standards (and hopes) are highest at the beginning of the night and wear down gradually as the night progresses.

Some guys will assess the situation and decide to blow the whole thing off and either just hang out with their (male) friends or say "screw the party" and go somewhere else—usually one of their favorite hangouts. The guys who end up staying for the duration are easy pickings later on, if you like—or if you want to ensure YOUR guy is not snatched up by some trollop.

This is where relationships get broken, arguments start, and people decide to "get what they can" to salvage the night (and their ego). If you have had your eye on a guy or two and they have not approached you at the party, now is the time to make your move.

The odds are in your favor that they will be so relieved to have a new (and pretty) face to talk to that they will be easily susceptible to any casual suggestions you decide to drop on them. This is a time-honored way of snagging that guy you were too nervous to go get before.

Various ways to get that cute guy interested in <u>you</u>

Better results, less effort on your part

While "individual tastes do vary," guys generally like girls who are any of the following. The more you can be on a daily basis, the more you can get guys to do things for you.

1: Feminine. Femininity is far more than your "physical looks." <u>Your personal femininity includes</u> your physical beauty, attitude toward men *(which is usually written all over your face)*, your manners *(politeness—or lack thereof, congeniality, etc.)*, how modest (or vain) you are publicly, your manner of dress *(Do you wear dresses? More and more women do not.)*, and your level of class.

NOTE: A lot of men like tomboys, so if you are not "built" overly-feminine, don't fret over that. *You will ALWAYS* catch more guys' attention by being yourself, and enjoying who you are, than you will by trying to be something that you are not. The beauty of being who-you-are inside is that the guys who really like "who you are" will be the ones most attracted to you.

24

2: Pretty (to them). Remember, while certain looks are generally popular, **every guy has his own individual tastes.** Five guys you meet today may find you "hot," and two others may ignore you altogether. Don't worry about impressing everyone. We (guys) even argue whether particular supermodels are "hot" or not. In fact, a lot of guys are turned off if "everyone else wants you." It becomes too much of a hassle, so we move on.

3: Charming. Okay, so your charm is part of your "femininity," but I wanted to mention it here to give it special emphasis. Our (American) culture has put the emphasis on visual appeal rather than politeness or warmth and charm.

That is because you can't put warmth and charm in a bottle and sell it. But pictures sell. Pictures are an easy way to transmit a message, so they "win." Because we have become so heavily reliant on images, we have, therefore, seen beauty more and more as "physical looks" alone (as in "pictures in magazines").

Men may act stupid, and some of us may even *be* stupid, <u>but we do know that having a pretty face does NOT mean that you have a pretty heart</u>. After one or two times of being blatantly screwed over by a woman (and most of us have been), we will learn, and become very distrustful of women in general. **Charm is the best way to counteract that.**

No matter how jaded a man is, he will forget every other woman and every bad experience he has ever had when a woman (any woman) successfully charms him. He will say to himself, "THIS WOMAN is the exception! This woman is *special.*" Charm a man and he will idealize you. The moment he idealizes you is the moment he separates you from all other women and puts you on a pedestal. Let him. Or at least let him enjoy his fantasy that "not all women are spawned from pure evil."

Charm school is gone and dead, but there are many good books (and magazines) that provide tips that have worked for women throughout the centuries. Old guys have a saying that they pass on to their younger counterparts. It goes like this:

"Don't reinvent the wheel dummy!"*

Learn from the old guys. The tricks that have worked for centuries still work (well the best ones still do). Your moms, aunts, and grandmothers, all had their own ways of attracting men. You are certainly not the first girl who ever had to deal with guys. If you can get quality advice from your (female) elders, great. If not, you might want to hit the library and rummage around through the older books to see what they have to say. Charm is your #1 tool for getting guys to do what you want—when you want it done. Your looks are secondary at best.

* You can ignore the "dummy" part. We (guys) like to insult each other *because it is fun.* Go figure.

4: In distress. (This lets the man "be a hero.") In more direct terms, it justifies his reason for being in *your* life, and has <u>the added benefit of making you *need him in your life*</u>. To a lot of men you will meet, the "fact" that you *need us* is a safety mechanism so that you will not leave us. This is why guys so readily take on the role of provider. If you *need* us, we feel that you are "not going anywhere," and that makes us feel more secure. The moment we see you overtly claiming your independence is when we get defensive, because we see that as a preparatory step to you leaving us (for some other guy of course).

<u>Too many guys are obsessed with "being needed"</u> and their role as provider. While a wounded sparrow is always easier to catch, some guys take this principle to such a degree that the women they date are literally held captive. Beware of the guy who wants you to be

26

too dependent upon him, most especially *financially*. This is usually a sign that he is secretly afraid of you leaving him (or of someone coming along that will treat you better). Watch for signs of any man trying to *contain* or *control* you.

It is accepted form to play the distress card as a way to get guys to help you, give you things, and generally get attention. Just be careful of getting caught up by a controlling jerk who will try to lock you away for his own pleasures. On a more positive note though, being "in need" of some (male) help gives a guy who WANTS to meet you an excuse to say "Hello." *In a perfect world* (like THAT will ever happen), no guy would ever be too insecure to walk right up to you and say hello. But we don't live in a perfect world, so it is up to you to make the best of it.

5: Easy going The only people who think that high maintenance women are sexy are high maintenance women, and stupid men who have zero self-esteem, no confidence, and think that they can't find anything better. The moment they do, however, they dump that high maintenance woman right on her well manicured ass. Moreover, there is a recent trend that says that "men like bitches." That is like saying that men like getting kicked in the groin. *Don't believe stupid lies.*

(Need I say more?)

6: Smiling. You smile at him. Simple as that. Read what I say about smiling in Section 3.

7: Cute. This is entirely optional. There is, of course, "beautiful" (Angelina Jolie) and then there is "cute" (that lady from the movie with the bus . . . Sandra Bullock). Cute does not mean "not beautiful," but it generally puts more focus on the personality. Cute goes well with "quirky" and "fun."

Are you a bit goofy, funny, strange, gothic, exotic, or any other flavor of different? If so, then you might be a breath of fresh air from the same cookie-cutter girls the guys around you see every day. If you have it—use it (to get guys to do what you want of course).

8: Interested in "Guy Things." Tomboys are cool. In fact, some of them are sexy in their own way. Do you know what a touchdown is? Okay, okay . . . so who won the very first Super Bowl? And which would you rather drive: a '65 convertible Mustang or a '56 Corvette? If you know this, you will have a serious edge over other women.

If you were raised with a handful of brothers, or for some reason you shied away from "girly" things, preferring hanging out with the guys, you can easily make this work for you. Balance your femininity with your comfortability with the guys and you will go further than most women ever do.

9: Athletic. Guys like girls who are not afraid to "break a nail." If you are active at all in sports (and figure skating does *not* count), especially sports a guy can compete with you in, then you will find guys looking for reasons to like you instantly, and that is a solid foundation for them wanting *to do things for you*.

Some ideas:

Some of the more exotic sports like archery, fencing *(yes, with swords)*, rowing, hang gliding, horseback riding, and bungee jumping are places to find more cultured guys (generally). These sports are not exactly "cheap," and tend not to attract "joe-sixpack" types.

Due to the fact that there will not usually be a lot of girls into these fun activities, you will more often than not *have the guys mostly to yourself.* You don't have to be "as good as every one of them," especially if you have been working on your charm and femininity (that was a pretty blatant hint). You will find that the guys, for the most part, scramble to find a balance between accepting you, impressing you, and looking out for you (see "in need" above). Lucky you.

Active sports such as snowboarding, skiing, football, volleyball (especially beach volleyball), skateboarding, even softball and soccer are good ways to meet guys *who are not couch potatoes.* They will probably have good bodies too. Don't worry. They will find ways to interact with you. Just be friendly and open (approachable). You can always blow off any idiots easily.

28

Poker. Hey! Poker "is too" a sport, if you believe the guys trying to get overweight, cigar smoking professional liars to be considered *Olympians*. Seriously: They are trying to make *poker* an Olympic sport, just like the *physical sports* (wrestling, boxing, gymnastics, swimming, ice skating, running, etc).

10: Famous and/or popular and/or powerful. Okay, okay, so *some guys* actually like women who can make "their life better." Male bimbos ("himbos") are more common than most people think. The biggest problem with them is that eventually they want to be taken seriously for some reason.

11: There. <u>If you are interested in a guy, but you go off somewhere else</u>, and some other girl is "there" (where he is), *guess who gets his attention?* Don't leave your guy alone too long or some other girl will try to steal him (if he is worth stealing). *Or just date higher in the gene pool.* Loyalty may be a virtue, but it is not taught in school. If you want loyalty, you have to look for it *up front* in the guys you want.

Rule #1:

Get *<u>his attention</u>* with your sex appeal,
smile, laugh, cuteness

(use whatever works at the moment).

Win *<u>him</u>* with your charm, wit,
and your <u>interest in him</u>.

Far too many women *put way too much emphasis* <u>on attracting men by arousing a man sexually</u>. This is of the school of thought that says, "Hey! Look at me! Me, me, me!! <u>I</u> am hot! Don't you want *me?*" That's like waving a steak in front of a hungry dog (hence the expression). The backlash to this approach is that sex becomes **the focus** of our desire. Of course we want sex—we are *men*. But if that is "all you have to offer," then that is all we will want from you, and that is how we will treat you (sorry—just the facts ma'am).

*If only it were
this easy in
real life . . .*

That method of attracting guys works just long enough to create resentment in men who realize that they are getting played <u>and will never have a chance with that woman</u>. **A better way** to get a man's attention—to see you as something special, different, and worth spending money on—is to show (even casual) interest *in him*.

Newsflash: Guys see beautiful women every day. We see them at work, walking down the street, on TV, and in magazines. Do we have sex with them? Um . . . no . . . These hot girls tend to lose their power over us over time. It's always fun to look, *but the bottom line is:* If there is <u>no possibility</u> of us getting affection from that woman, <u>she will get nothing from us but a glance</u> (and maybe a few choice words she may not like at the time).

It's no secret that (all but a few) men want *action*. We thrive on "doing," not "talking," or "planning." We like to jump right into something and *mix it up*. This makes us easy prey for any girl who can show us the promise of (overtly implied possibility of) her affection. While one girl is busy playing "hard to get" or "making us wait," we are having fun with her friend who is more relaxed about going out and having a good time. This doesn't mean that we are having sex with her friend (not in every instance). It means that the girl who knows how to <u>use her charm and femininity to hold our attention</u> "wins." *Always*.

So the "reasonably attractive girl" who smiles at us, seems to want to know who we are, is not overly demanding, *and might just care about us as people*, <u>hooks us easily</u>—like a fish. Hell, we will even jump right into the boat and flop around! How you look to him is only 30% of what it takes to hold a man's attention longer than it takes him to fantasize about you. Even if you are a supermodel in a bikini, you *must* smile at the guy and seem genuinely interested in him, even if it is only mildly so, to get and hold his attention long enough for you to see what he is about—who he is.

Men see pretty women all-day-long, *every day of the week.* We are inundated with images of women on billboards, TV, and the covers of magazines. All of these promise "beauty" to us if we just buy whatever products they are hawking. The effect of this is rather numbing, and more than a bit disenchanting, as the whole of it drives the message into men's heads that women (especially the most physically attractive ones) will not give us a moment's worth of their time unless we spend money (on _____). This constant barrage of programming leads directly to animosity toward women, especially ones who "won't give you the time of day."

Since most men are used to receiving extremely subtle "don't look at me, don't touch me, don't talk to me" messages from women on a regular basis, they are easy marks for a smile or a casual "hello." Your personality, attitude towards him, chemistry, and circumstance all make up the other 70% of stealing his interest away from anyone and everything else, and locking it onto you.

In addition to your smile, you have several other ways to drop a man's defenses in any situation. You can establish control of your interaction with almost any guy just by the use of your body language, carefully selected perfume, choice of words, the tone of your voice, *the way and how long you look at him,* your touch, and your attitude towards him when you first see him.

These are just as important as the dress you wear. With a little practice, you will realize just how easy it is to wrap any man around your finger. It is so easy that is it downright obscene. As a rule, men are taught that it is "manly" to see "the big picture" and *focus on the end-goal,* and that details are secondary to victory and other such nonsense. This gender-specific brainwashing affects all of us, and has been a part of society since the beginning of time. But it is also a giant blinking sign that points to a huge weakness men, in general, have:

In their mad dash *to impress you,* all the way to the bedroom, men don't consciously realize how much <u>they are affected by</u> the quality of your voice, the sound of your laugh, how you smell, *whether you touch them,* where and how you touch them, <u>and how much you do.</u> Men are not taught to understand the effects your femininity has on them; so these signals usually slip right past their awareness and start to work directly on their emotions.

If you use all of these tools of influence subtly, the effect is that men end up thinking that "there is something special about you," something they cannot put their finger on (because details are for wimps—a *real man* just muscles his way through problems until they are fixed—don't think that your man is immune to this). **They will stop thinking of you as an object and start thinking of you as a person they want around them.**

This sets you apart from the crowds of women they just want to see naked, and touch a lot. Even if you think guys "don't hear a word you say," they are picking up subtle clues subconsciously and reading into them. Most of the time they have no idea that all of this interaction is going on. This is because, as a rule, men are programmed to ignore all of this—and think only of various parts of your body. You really have to love the power of marketing. Let your men get lost in you. Their obsession with you will blind them to your subtle machinations.

Secrets from the Mystery School 101: The power of feminine sexual attraction on a man is the single most potent drug in existence. It has throughout time (and will continue to) created the best advancements in society and caused the worst destruction the world has seen. But alone it is like a match flame. It fires up easily enough but is quickly extinguished by the winds of circumstance. It is a mere spark to something far more enduring, and used improperly it fails to generate its full potential. This impulse must mesh with deeper bonds to create greatness. By encouraging the growth and development of subtle bonds between you and the men you want in your life, you build a level of influence on them unattainable by other means, <u>no matter how much effort</u> you invest. This works on the men in your life, and it works on you; and it is one of the secrets of manifesting the dreams you want to come true in your life. More at: ***www.EnlightenedSisterhood.net.***

In a guy's mind . . .
The perfect date

Age 15

Girl's parents drop her off.

Girl kisses you after telling you how "hot" you look tonight.

Have fun showing off what a "man" you are, much to the girl's amazement and joy.

Get through the night without doing something stupid, or some other guy stealing your girl.

Age 21

Girl shows up at party; starts drinking heavily.

Girl laughs at all of your stupid jokes—doesn't flirt with your friends.

Hopefully, get some sex before date ends, *uninterrupted by your idiot friends.*

Do a good enough job to impress her so she will want more soon.

Age 30

Pick up girl in limo.

Woman is impressed by how rich, handsome, witty, and/or sexy you are.

Woman seduces you—making you feel like you are sexier than any other man she has been with.

Good sex—or at least she fakes it so well that you think you "rocked her world."

Age 50+

Woman actually shows up for the date.

Attracting Men

What works:	**What doesn't:**
Get his attention, make eye contact, and smile (at him).	Pay no attention to him. *Make him work for it.*
Look him in the eye. You can always look away later.	Pay attention to his friend(s).
Make yourself approachable. Put some open space around you, send your friend to get something for you, so you will be alone for a moment or two, or *you get up and walk to the other side of the room (passing by the guy you want to meet).*	Figure that you are attractive enough that the cutest or best guys will come talk to you.
	Surround yourself with your friends (like a force field that stops men from approaching your group).
If he does not approach you, get up and go say hello to him. Ask him an innocuous question, or compliment him on something he is either doing or wearing. Let nature take its course. **If you get bored, _walk away_.**	Talk excessively loud. Too many girls do this. It chases most decent men away because it usually makes you look like an attention whore.
	Have an attitude. *Make sure that everyone knows you do.* After all, "hot guys love bitches!"

Depending on your potential interest in a guy,

<u>hold eye contact</u>:

- Less than a second if you just want to check him out. Don't look at him again for a few seconds if you can help it.

- One to two seconds if you want him to come talk to you.

- Anything longer than two seconds and you might as well hold up a sign for him.

- Repeat as necessary (no more than twice).

Sadly enough though, <u>some men just don't get the hint,</u> or they are too shy, distracted, glued to their seat by one of their friends as a practical joke *(which is unbelievably fun by the way),*

. . . married, or just too drunk to stand up and too polite to fall on you in the process of trying to.

If the guy looks interesting enough, take a chance and say hello to him. You aren't asking him to have sex with you in the parking lot *(are you?)*. You are just saying "hello." So there is no pressure on you.

One of the easiest ways to break the ice with a complete stranger is to compliment them on something they are doing, wearing, reading, or comment on something you overheard them say. This trick is older than time, but there are two interesting facts you should always remember:

1: It always works, especially on guys. This simple trick has the added benefit of acting as a psychosis barometer. If you smile and say a casual "hello" in passing, or approach and offer a light compliment to a guy, allowing him to take the cue and spark up the conversation, and he turns out to be a bore, you can dump him off easily enough (see details in this book). Besides, it's best that you find these things out before you waste your time and/or money on any guy. Best of all, **this little trick puts you in charge.** You get to pick out who you will meet (and size up) rather than waiting around for "Mr. Right" to find you. After all, if he was going to find you (and not your best friend), he would have done so by now, right? *Screw the frogs!* Go find your prince!

2: Even people who know this completely forget how to do it when they see someone they want to meet. The idea of offering a complete stranger a friendly compliment has gone out of style in our society. There is so much endemic paranoia over crime, terrorism, *or even germs,* that we have isolated ourselves from each other. The result is that we have collectively forgotten how to meet people, and we need dating services or websites just to say hello to anyone.

This is why guys resort to stupid pick-up lines when meeting women. They have not been taught by their parents, teachers, or friends how to casually approach women. To most men, *romance has become an act of buying something that will impress you* enough to "like him." The general consensus among men is that the more expensive the gift, dinner, or vacation, the more impressed you will be with him as a person.

You can learn a lot about the general makeup of a guy in your first few minutes of conversation with him. Look past any compliments he hands you and see what he is really saying. Does he spend his opening minutes telling you how "hot you are" or "how hot he is"? Does he try to impress you with *his* skills, accomplishments, or physical abilities? A guy who meets you and wants to impress you will almost always show you what he prides himself in, or he will go straight for the manipulation tactic: turning the focus on you, and how/why you need him to tell/show you what to do (in life, tonight, however long it takes to get to the back seat . . .). This is your clue as to what to expect overall in your interactions with him.

It is easy when first meeting anyone (especially the ones who really catch your eye) to get caught up in the moment and miss what is being said. Do his words and actions subtly show a respect, even a reverence for you, or is he sending clear signals that you are "less than him" and "lucky to be in his presence"? Don't ignore these signals or you will be spending the next few weeks or months complaining to your friends how "he did this or that to you."

By closely paying attention to the first few minutes (or hours) of meeting any guy, you can get an instant feel for how he will treat you over time. Pay attention *before* he decides to change his tactic, and makes it harder to see behind the facade that we all enact when trying to impress someone new.

HOW TO MEET HOT GUYS!

Approaching them,
getting them to approach <u>you</u>
(on your terms of course).

First:

Smile

 I said, <u>smile</u>!

Okay, that's good.
Now smile more . . .

 *Great! Let's go meet some hot guys!*

If at first a cute guy doesn't approach you, don't wait for him to spot some other girl, walk up to him and say hello.

Hi!

. . . or spill your drink on him.

You might accidentally step *(gently)* on his foot . . .

Bump into him (make him apologize first, then say it was your fault).

But <u>do not approach his friend</u> trying to get closer *to him*.

How to get a guy to approach you so you can find out if you like him enough to actually talk to him

The following is fairly basic, time-tested stuff, but it works. And too many people seem to have forgotten how to flirt. So here is a quickie refresher course: (I hope you like quickies.)

1: Get his attention.

2: Make eye contact <u>and smile</u> (at him).

3: Look away.

4: Repeat as necessary (no more than twice).

"Be approachable"

Are you "surrounded" by friends? Too many friends happily chatting away sends a message that *you do NOT want to be interrupted* by some guy looking for a date. Are you talking on your cell phone? Is your nose buried in a book or magazine? These are all walls that keep away *all but the most persistent of* men (usually the professional players—any good pick-up book teaches men how to hit on three or more women in a group). If you want to meet a guy, you have to be available or he will look around to see if there is someone else who is.

What to do if that doesn't work

1: Get up and walk over to him.

2: On your way over, think of something innocuous or compelling to say to him.

3: *Casually* compliment him on something he is doing or wearing, ask him a question, or just say hello.

4: <u>Let him impress you</u> with his conversational skills. Turn around and walk away if you get bored.

Why? Why? Why?

Most guys are easy. If you talk to them, they will talk to you, unless there is something wrong with them (in which case you simply toss them back into the dating pool for some other fish to catch).

Guys miss subtleties. Sometimes a guy is just too wrapped up in something to recognize the "hey, come talk to me" signs you are tossing out at him. Other times the guy might have just accidentally hit on someone else's wife and is a bit hesitant about making *that* mistake again. His dog died, he won't get paid until tomorrow and is running short on cash, he is an introvert . . .

However, you will almost never see a guy playing "hard to get" (unless he is so oversexed that he really doesn't care about you at all—but you would figure that out in the first 30 seconds of talking to him anyway). If you catch a guy pretending that he is not interested in you because he is "important" or some kind of celebrity, *take that immediately as a red flag that you are being maneuvered into a position that is easier to manipulate.*

If you see a guy you want to meet (long enough to figure out if you want to keep talking to him), and he hasn't made a move, you have a choice: either you go up to him and say something *or you never* meet him. He may be a total loser or a millionaire. It's getting harder to tell us apart these days *until you say hello to us* and see what we say back. If the guy is a bum, toss him back into the pool.

Sometimes the best guys are the last ones you meet. Think about this for a moment. Usually the guys who blatantly hit on you have the least going for them. The reason you aren't hit on by cute millionaires every day is because they are usually too busy becoming millionaires to spend all day harassing random women. This is also why you haven't met that starving artist or actor who next year will be internationally famous—*and* rich. And forget self-help authors—they are completely useless. But by and large, the men who live their lives <u>with passion</u> are usually out living their lives with passion.

<u>Now, this is not to say that</u> every guy who hits on you has nothing going for him. Not at all. The point you need to get here is that we all have the same 24 hours a day to work with, and as guys we

have some hard choices to make in life: go find women to ask out, hang out with our friends, watch TV, play Xbox or PSP, or get drunk so that we can forget our crappy jobs for a few hours. We couldn't fit all of those into a day planner.

If you are looking for someone who will be rich, famous, or "really do something big with their lives," then you have to realize that "that guy" has all of the above to do and another 4–6 hours every day of working on his passions in life. When you see him, he may be so busy trying to squeeze three things (see above list) into one night that he completely misses you.

He sees you, smiles, thinks "Wow" (or something similar), and perhaps seeing you gives him a brilliant idea. The next thing you know his brain is off working on the idea instead of trying to get your phone number. (Oops!) Six months later, he is on the cover of TIME magazine, and *you never know that <u>you were his Mona Lisa</u>*.

Here's a creepier version of that same scenario:

Sometimes the guys you want to meet will miss your subtle "come talk to me" clues. This is because the guys you are looking for *are not the ones who are observing you from across the room,* looking for weaknesses, listening to every word you say, while planning on how to use your words to manipulate you into doing what they want.

While the "decent guys" are <u>standing there like idiots</u>, a player *(who has been watching you, looking for weaknesses)* approaches you and tells you everything he knows you want to hear. A week later your "friend" shows up with her new boyfriend—that hot guy that was too stupid to come talk to you. It turns out that he is a really nice guy, kinda shy at first, and he's a med student. Oh, and as to that player who hit on you at the party last week: You haven't seen him since.

<u>You can avoid all of this</u> by simply finding ways to walk up to guys you want to meet. (In fact, I have several techniques outlined in this book.) Find out whether you want to know them before assuming that if they don't talk to you, they are not worth your time. The worst that will usually happen is that you end up making

a lot of guy "friends" (and you can never have too many friends). By the way: "Decent guys" often come across as complete idiots during the first few minutes of meeting them.

There is no class in school on "how to talk to girls," and most books for guys on "how to pick up girls" tell guys to brainwash you into thinking that you are horny for them, not good enough for them (and *why you should feel lucky* to be demeaned by them), or teach the guys stupid techniques to use to trick you into liking them. *If you doubt me,* read a few books on "how to pick up girls." You will be amazed at what guys are being taught. Unless you take charge of your own destiny (and relationships), the odds are that you will be extremely dissatisfied by the men in your life.

Other than what guys learn in locker rooms, guys usually learn from trial and error. Of course, this means that every time a guy makes an idiot of himself, the idea of *doing that* again makes him stop and try to think of an easier way to get girls to notice him. Guys don't get nearly enough practice approaching women to become very good at it. This is why "God" invented pick-up lines. If it weren't for pick-up lines, a lot of men would never talk to women.

If the guy is cute enough (to you), and you get a good feel from him, give him some time and help him show you who he really is by helping him to relax, as if you two were already friends. Listen attentively and show interest in what he is "all about." Loosen your stance so that your posture is relaxed and he will follow suit. As his defenses drop, so will his pretenses, and you will begin to see *exactly who he is,* without him realizing that he is unconsciously showing you what he is like when he is not on his best behavior trying to impress someone new.

His mannerisms will reveal his true personality (who he is every day), even against his conscious will. If he is normally very aggressive or assumptive with women, you will catch on real fast—before you get too involved with him. If he is casual, laid-back, assertive, or indecisive by nature, all of this will start to show almost immediately.

Remember: *The more you get someone to relax in your company, the more they will show you who they are and, thus, the better you will be able to spot the people worth knowing.*

This works on everyone—even you.

In fact, this technique works extremely well on professional PUA's (pick-up artists). All but the very best of them will mistake your relaxed nature as a sign of an easy conquest and move in for the kill fast. You can play him for as long as you like, or simply dump him off after you have had a good laugh.

The male ego is a powerful thing, _and the more you make it work for you,_ the easier it is to get what you want from men without ANY arguments. Keep in mind that most arguments that men have with women start and end with the guy's perceptions _that the woman has attacked their ego or denied them affection._

By making a man feel empowered _(important, "special," sexy, appreciated, handsome, respected, loved—pick any one of these)_ for doing what YOU want him to do, you (like Delilah) can get him to do just about anything you like. More on this in Section 3.

Using a friend to "go talk to that guy for me"

The problem with this is that guys will end up bonding with the girl who they feel comfortable talking to; _which is usually the one who approaches them and says, "Hi!"_ If that is your friend (instead of you), where does that leave you? Unless you are at least twice as attractive as your "friend" (and what kind of friend is she anyway if she will steal your men?) AND you have a decent personality (from a guy's point of view), you are asking for trouble having your friends fetch guys for you.

5 reasons why you should approach guys you want to meet _(and find out from there if you want to know them for very long)_

1: It puts you in control. Why in the world would you wait for some guy to decide that _you are worth talking to?_ Think about this for a moment: Guys notice you every day. If you get out at all (school, the mall, Starbucks—I think you get the idea), guys will notice. *It is what we do.* We have radar. Of course, a really hypnotic perfume helps in case you are behind us, but in general you should know that if you go anywhere, any time, at least 50 guys will check you out (even momentarily) *every single day.*

If you are waiting for a guy to approach you, what you are doing is letting random chance decide what guys you will meet. Let me give you an example of what you are doing to yourself. If you have a deck of cards, you can play along at home. The following example is amazingly accurate:

Let's say I was your matchmaker (and for a very expensive fee, I can be). I have a deck of cards representing 52 men you can meet on any given day. Out of the 52 cards, only 4 of them are kings, and another 4 are princes (future kings—if you like fixer uppers). These 8 cards are your "perfect men," your potential soul mates—let's hope you draw one of these so I can get paid and go home early. The rest are average guys, ranging from complete assholes to fairly decent "nice guys" that may or may not be "just your type." Let's see, 52 cards (or men), minus the 8 you would really like the best, and that leaves 44 men of quality ranging from "okay" to horrific.

That means that your chances of actually meeting a guy you will go crazy for **_are 1 in 13_** (not very good really), or 2 in 13 if you don't mind fixing him up (which usually sounds a LOT easier than it actually is when you try doing it to your boyfriend).

But wait! *It gets worse!* As mentioned earlier, guys with <u>anything</u> going for them usually have most of their time consumed by the very thing that makes them so great. For example, a rock star is usually practicing or performing, and an artist is creating art. It is the guys with boring day jobs and no real passion that have all the time in the world to go out and try to impress any girl they can. So, instead of your odds being 1 (or 2) in 13 of meeting a guy worthy of obsessing over—by waiting for him to find you—your odds are more like zero. Otherwise, you would have met him already.

You will meet (on a regular basis) guys who disappoint you once you realize that other than a nice smile, car, or pick-up line, they really don't have that much going for them. In the meantime, the guys you WANT to meet are busy living a life you can only dream of, with some girl who snagged them.

If the current system of dating *actually worked,* everyone would be happy. Relationships would be great, and we would all be with the "one person" (or several) who made us the happiest. There would be no abusive relationships, no "cheating," divorce, no broken hearts. The way to fix YOUR love life is to decide exactly what you want in a guy (or what kind of guy you want) <u>and go get one</u>.

Don't be afraid to try a few on for size.

Think of guys as shoes . . .
How boring would life be
if you were "assigned" shoes?

Everywhere you go, shoes picked you, instead of you getting to pick out which shoes you wanted to try on. *Oh no! Here comes a pair of size 3 work boots!* They are too small and cramp your toes (and your style), but they keep pestering you. <u>Shoes you have absolutely no interest in</u> start closing in on you trying to get you to take them home.

Do you think you would ever end up with $1,200 Jimmy Choos or a new pair of perfect-fitting, Salvatore Ferragamo shoes? **Hardly.** You would more than likely be hit on by every cheap pair of sneakers that crossed your path. Even if an expensive pair of shoes you had your eye on decided to approach you, they would have to fight their way past all of the cheap knockoffs <u>pretending</u> to be quality shoes.

Meeting guys is no different. If you think you can beat the odds, *keep waiting for "Mr. Right" to come along.* Naturally, the moment he gets close, one of your "friends" will throw herself at him just in time to stop him from meeting you. This happens to women every day, all over the world. In the meantime, "Mr. Well-I-can't-find-anything-better" will be more than happy to waste your 20's, 30's, even 40's. By the time you finally do meet "Mr. Right," he will already be married *(and so might you).*

Or . . . you can stop wasting time with jerks, losers, poseurs, players, pimps, and assholes. Decide what you want and go get him. All you have to do is smile and say "Hello." After all, would you rather spend the next year being hit on by guys you have absolutely no interest in or spend the next year with guys who really turn you on?

2: <u>It surrounds you with a wall of guys you want to meet</u>, which is the best defense against having jerks and weirdos constantly "Hey baby"-ing you to death. Imagine: No more getting cornered by creepy guys, while you scan the room desperately wishing for a cute guy or a friend to come rescue you.

3: <u>It will make you more popular than you can possibly imagine</u>. Let's say tomorrow you start your new life approaching guys you want to meet. Within a week you will easily have 5–25 new friends. Whether you spend a few minutes talking to the guy and decide "friend," "acquaintance," or "Next!!," you win. *You build your confidence easily and quickly,* and you end up with a lot of guys who like you enough to hold a spot in line for you, give you a ride, or beat up some jerk for you. Some of your new "friends" will even buy you stuff, without even asking.

4: "Hello" is *not* a secret code for "Wanna have sex?" When you say hello to a guy, you are doing what most girls he sees on any given day would never think of doing. While they are all waiting for some cute guy to notice them, you are grabbing his attention. You are just making a new friend; how simple is that? Being a guy, he will start considering how interested he is (or could become) in you. That is nature doing its job. Be sure to read the section on "How to say hello to guys without looking like you are trying to pick up on them." Some of the most fun guys to date won't approach you for any number of reasons. *This doesn't mean that the guys who do approach you are boring,* but just because a guy hits on you doesn't mean that he is any good for you—or will treat you well. Don't wait for some guy *you want to meet* to notice you. Pick up something and throw it at him (a football works nicely in most cases). Meet him before someone else does.

5: If you *don't* walk up and say hello to him, <u>you may end up meeting him as "your friend's new boyfriend."</u> What if he turns out to be the guy you always wanted?

How to have the <u>confidence</u>
to approach cute guys
you want to meet

<u>Confidence comes easily</u>. It is *lack of confidence* that takes a while to develop. **We are all born with confidence.** Think back to when you were a kid and how much trouble you got into because you "did" things. As a kid there was never a question of whether or not you "could" get a cookie (if you could find them); if you wanted a cookie, you simply went on a cookie hunt or asked mom for a cookie (which hopefully worked more often than not).

<u>We had to *learn* to hesitate</u> and we usually learned only after being told "a thousand times" *not* to do something.

Life is great when you are 3. There is almost nothing you can't do. Four is where everything grinds to a halt, and the word "no" finally sets in. That nefarious word "no" is as tenacious as it is limiting. Once you finally learn to doubt yourself, the habit does its best to become a lasting part of your psyche—kinda like a ketchup stain—good luck getting *that* out. Fortunately for you, we just so happen to have a few bottles of Psyche Scrub™ gathering dust in the back. "We will get rid of any mental stains you want gone in 30 seconds or less!"

To remove any stains of self-doubt when it comes to approaching guys, we (you and I) will start by identifying what you are already confident about. We all have talents that we feel comfortable doing, so much so that we tend to downplay them and even believe that *anyone can do them.*

No matter how hard we have worked on maximizing these talents, when someone compliments our skills, it is often easier for us to believe that our talents are nothing special. Once we master a task, we tend to devalue our accomplishment and look to new challenges. We wish for other talents we admire, but have not yet mastered. This is the nature of confidence. This is where we will start looking.

Spend a few minutes thinking about what you are naturally good at. If you can't think of anything else, we will start with breathing. After all, you have to be very good at breathing or else you wouldn't be reading this. And what about reading? And walking, sleeping . . . why there are a whole lot of things you are extremely proficient at—so much so that you never even stop to think about them.

". . . so much so that you never even stop to think about them."

C-o-n-f-i-d-e-n-c-e
starts with
NOT t-h-i-n-k-i-n-g

C'mon, how many guys have you dated (or do you know) <u>that have complete confidence</u> about something that you _know_ they have absolutely no skill in?

Think about the old cliché about guys not stopping to ask for directions because they're c-o-n-f-i-d-e-n-t that they can figure out how to get to where they are going. YOUR problem is that you actually think things through. YOU need a map. We (guys) don't need a map—because a map requires t-h-i-n-k-i-n-g. It also requires us to admit that we are lost.

When you "really want a triple mocha Frappuccino," you don't stand at the Starbucks counter asking yourself _if_ you can speak English. But when you are confronted with the prospect of marching over to that hot guy you like and striking up a conversation with him, suddenly you forget how to string words together coherently.

This happens to guys all the time. We think it's great fun. It's downright hilarious to watch one of our buddies walk up to you and forget his own name. Then we get to "school him" on what he should have done, because it is always easier to watch a situation and comment on what everyone involved should have done than it is to actually get up and go do it. But it's time for you to leave the sudden "lack of confidence" to the guys. Here's how to have instant confidence in _any_ situation you ever find yourself in:

The first thing you need to do is to take a breath and **stop overthinking everything.** The moment you see a cute guy you want to meet, remember, <u>all you really want to do is</u> find out if you still like him after listening to him for 5 minutes. That takes the pressure off of you, _and puts it on him._ So he's cute, wealthy, popular—whatever . . .

Thirty seconds after you say hello
<u>you will have forgotten who said</u> hello

You will be sizing him up, deciding whether or not he still impresses you now that you have his full attention. How many famous, powerful, or popular people have you admired, and then met, that turned out to be a real disappointment once you saw what they were like in person? This guy could turn out to be a complete bore.

The worst thing that could happen is that you do nothing. Suddenly your best friend shows up, sees you and starts over to say hello, trips and spills her mocha Frappuccino all over him, she apologizes, he says it's no problem, their eyes meet . . . Three months later you are a bridesmaid at their wedding—oh, this is *after* you found out that the guy is totally the guy of your dreams.

Wow . . . that sucks!

Okay, let's try this again—before your "friend" saunters in with her guy of your dreams stealing antics. You see this guy and catch yourself wishing he would come over and say "Hi." Just long enough for you to see if you like talking to him as much as you like looking at him.

But wait, he's glancing over at Becky, who already has a boyfriend (and why should she have two—and you have "none" anyway?). Well, you are about to work up the nerve to walk up and "accidentally" spill *your* mocha Frappuccino on him when that creepy guy who has been stalking you all week starts heading your way.

That's it. You *leap* out of your seat and almost trip over yourself on your way to hide behind the cute guy, hoping that he isn't friends with creepy-stalker-guy. You bump into him (the cute guy) by mistake and he stops ogling that tramp Becky and glances at you. Before you can think, you have said "Oops!" and "Hi." He says hello back and looks at you for a moment. Wow . . . that was hard.

Now open your mouth and make a noise. Any noise will do, especially if it sounds something like "Hey do you know what time it is?," followed by "That's a nice/cool watch," or possibly "I hate to be a burden, but you look kinda strong, and there is a guy I think is stalking me—would you mind terribly walking me to my car?"

In fact, you could say just about anything that comes to mind. You have a decided advantage, in that you are female. You can ask a guy for help, what time it is, or compliment him on something he is doing or wearing (more on all of this in a moment) with no pressure on you. His reaction will tell you immediately a lot more about him than if you waited for him to approach you.

Most guys will be a bit surprised, but happy to start up a short conversation with you, if they find you even remotely attractive, unless they are in a relationship (and their girlfriend just happens to be on the way back from the bathroom) or they are preoccupied with something at the moment. The last thing he will be thinking is that you are hitting on him, unless you make it obvious that you are—or he is a professional womanizer. The point is that most guys you approach casually will be happy to say hello and talk for a bit while the two of you figure out if you can stand each other.

What to say first: (try them all!)
(Guaranteed to work wonders for you!*)

1: **Hello.**

2: **I've been stalking you all night and you still haven't said hello to me!** Then laugh.

3: **You dropped this.** Hand him a dollar.

4: (If he's really cute) **You dropped this.** Hand him a condom.

5: (At the office) **How do you work this thing?** (hand him an open stapler and a rack of staples)

6: **Hey you look pretty strong; can you help me with this please?** No one says please anymore, so catch him off guard with your smile and manners.

7: **Wow, what a cute dog** (cat, ferret, baby . . .). **What's his/her name?**

8: (This works best at a party.) **So are you going to buy me a drink, or do I have to buy you one?** Then laugh.

9: **Oops!** (Bump into him. Then ask if he is all right.)

10: *(Anywhere he is watching sports on TV)* Sidle up somewhat close to him and ask casually, **"What's the score?"** while looking at the TV. Glance at him briefly *after you ask,* then back at the TV. Glance back at him again momentarily when he answers. He will pick up from there.

11: **You busy?** If you do this, have a strong follow-up request or suggestion. Stay in control by being funny or suggestive, but state your request with an authority that entices his agreement.

12: **Is this seat taken?** If he can't open a conversation after you sit next to him, he is hopelessly shy, or happily married.

13: **Is that _____ you are reading?** (or) **Is that a _____?** (Let him explain all about it.)

14: **What time is it?/Hey, I used to have that watch . . .** *(just lie)*

15: Walk up to a cute guy and look him in the eye, pause a moment and casually say, **"You're standing on my foot."** Wait half a second while he looks down and laugh. If he laughs too, he is yours.

16: Assuming that both of you smoke; look him directly in the eye, smile slightly and ask him, **"Got a light?"** This really works best if you walk up to him, *drop your reasonably freshly lit cigarette, step on it, and fish out a new one before asking him.* If you perfect this one, you can leave a man speechless as he fumbles for his lighter, desperately trying to think of something "cool" to say to you.

All of these opening lines are designed to get his attention without putting you in a position where you owe him anything (a favor, an explanation, 5 minutes of your time . . .). They are fun ways to break the ice and decide by his response(s) if you want to get to know him better or not. All you are doing is getting his attention, and making it easy for him to respond and strike up a conversation wherein *you get to decide* if you have any real interest in him.

* Like most guarantees, this one is scheduled to run out five minutes before you actually try any of these.

The more you practice this, the better you will become and the more attention you will get. You can check out guys all day long, at your convenience, and still have time for everything else in your day planner. The worst that could possibly happen is that you will have a ton of new male friends and become very adept (very quickly) at blowing off boring guys without them ending up feeling rejected (see page 82). **Remember:** *You can never have <u>too many</u> "guy" friends to help you out of a jam at some point.*

What to say next

Leave the boring conversation to girls <u>that rely on their looks to get guys interested in them</u>. Even if you think you "are all that," being fun, funny, and/or original will cement you in a guy's mind. This *will make the difference* between him looking to have sex with you and brag to all of his friends and him actually wanting to spend time with you. *The quality of your character and personality will set you apart* from any other girl he meets in the next week (or three, if you are really good). Just a few words when you first meet any guy can make all the difference in how much he respects you, wants to impress you, <u>and definitely how much of his time and money he will spend on you</u>. Stop being "an object" (hot chick) **and you become something that every guy fights/drools over** (*cool, fun, likable* hot chick).

Since we are on the subject, let me nag you about remembering something most girls will never, ever understand about guys: Being friendly, fun, cool, interesting, easy going, etc., will *instantly add 1–2 "points" on your rating (on a scale of 1 to 10)*. In other words, if you are a "6" or a "7," you can easily become an "8," or even a "9" to some guys, <u>simply by working on your personality</u>. Being a self-centered bitch (if you need an example, pick any <u>openly narcissistic</u> celebrity—there are always a few to choose from) **will DROP you from a "9" to a "6"** to most guys faster than anything else you can possibly do, *so* **be nice**. *(Not "easy," or "weak," a pushover, spineless, or dumb—just "nice.")* Boundaries work when you establish them early along with the bonds you are creating. This is so important that I want you to come back and read this page every week for the next 6 months. Go ahead and fold it now, so you do not forget. Okay, enough of this rant. Here are a few fun ideas of what to say at this point.

If he is offended by your opening line, try this:

"It was a joke."   . . . *or*

"I'm sorry, I am new to your planet. Was that in bad taste?"
(Small laugh)   . . . *or*

"I'm sorry, your friend told me to say that. (Smile) Hi, I'm _____."

If he comes on too strong:

"It was a joke. Excuse me, I have to get some punch." This works especially well if you are not at a party or anyplace where there is obviously no "punch." Leave him confused.   . . . *or*

"You know, I appreciate the offer, but the delivery is all wrong . . . Hmmm . . . This is a bit much for me. Excuse me, I have to go now."

If he laughs at your joke:

Say, "Thank you," smile, and tell him that you ran out of jokes and that was all you had left.   . . . *or*

Say excitedly, "Okay, now it's your turn!" (to tell you a joke)
. . . *or*

"So . . . Come here often?" Then laugh at the absurdity of using such a cheesy pick-up line. Get him to respond.

If he doesn't laugh at your joke:

Pout and say that you just read in a magazine that this joke was guaranteed to make any man laugh. Ask him if he has a joke.

Or look at him in mock disbelief and say, "Hey! That joke cost me five bucks!" Then lean in just a bit and ask in a conspiratorial tone, *"You wouldn't have a spare joke on you, would you?"*

57

Section 3

Guys:

How to get them
to do what you want!

Rule #2:

Men don't want a woman __who is smart__, politically correct, or powerful . . . They "want" a woman who thinks __they__ are a-m-a-z-i-n-g!!

Don't "fake it." Find something about him that you can obsess over: some part of him that makes him irresistible to you. Keep your individuality—your specific personality that is you—and express your admiration for him through that. Do not become something or someone else in the process. The more you change for someone, the more you will end up feeling empty, as if you "lost something" in life, *and hating them for it.*

What makes men do *what you want* is your ability to fan the flames of their natural urges, and make them feel better for doing what it is that you want them to do. This requires practice, finesse, and subtlety. History is littered with countless examples of men who have created and destroyed monuments, empires, started (or fought in) wars, and undertaken great adventures—all over the affection (or lack thereof) of a woman.

These women knew the secrets of persuasion that I am revealing here. There is nothing written in this book that has not changed the course of history many times over. Nothing contained in these pages is beyond your grasp, and most of it you should know already. *But knowing and doing with a purpose are two completely different things.*

You can read this book several times over, and it will not do you any good until you actually use these techniques to get men to do what you want. **It is your application of these techniques that will decide both your future, and the future of the world.**

Your life can be anything you desire it to be. You have at your disposal all of the power of your own mind, your physical capabilities, and the efforts of any man you bend to your will. This is how it is, how it has always been, and how it will be until men invent a substitute for women.

If you continue to do what you have always done,
you will get the results you have always gotten.

The choice is yours really: Struggle to get the life you want, relying solely on your own efforts, or have an army of guys *helping you* get everything you want in life.

Quick: What do "average men" and Superman™ have in common?

Um . . . well . . . okay . . . nothing really *(sorry)*. But properly applied femininity is like Kryptonite to your average man. Superman can stop bullets, jump tall buildings, hide his identity in a flash simply by slipping on a pair of black-rimmed glasses, *but he is powerless to a small handful of green-glowing rocks* from his hometown.

Average men can stop at a bar after work for a drink, leap out of their seats faster than a speeding bullet every time their team scores a touchdown, and are more powerful than a locomotive full of beer . . . Well, they can *unload* a locomotive full of beer, *but they are powerless to the right woman's femininity.* Your innate sexuality is intoxicating, enticing, and threatening to any man who finds you at all attractive. It is our greatest goal, and our greatest enemy.

"Don't worry . . .
It's not you.
It's me."

It is not your sexuality that men fear. It is the thought of you sharing your sexuality *with any other man,* especially a man who is wealthier, more attractive, a better lover, and any other number of real and imagined fears we can conjure up.

Once a man establishes emotional interest in you, the imagined threat of another man coming along and stealing you away from him can be so disempowering (depending on how wrapped up in you he is) that men everywhere have come up with various ways **to prevent that from happening.**

Because we know (think) that some other guy will be more than happy to "pay your way through life," we feel (put) pressure on ourselves to ensure that you do not take your love from us, and give it to someone else. Yeah, yeah, I know this makes absolutely no sense, but it is how the male mind works. This should answer any number of questions you've had about "why guys do the things they do."

What I want you to get from this is the power of *negative motivation*. There are more than enough books on negative motivation, so I will not add to their number. **I want you to see how using positive motivational techniques on the men in your life will make your life infinitely easier,** *and a lot more fun.*

Take some time and think about this.

*Talk it over with some of
your more level-headed friends.*

<u>*It will change your life*</u>.

Turning Heads
versus
Capturing Hearts

The difference between sex appeal and charm
– and –
how to work <u>both</u> on men to get what you want

So much emphasis is placed on "being sexy" in today's culture that it seems a good time for a refresher course in capturing hearts. "Being sexy" is nice and all that, but what good does it really do if guys just want to have sex with you—and want nothing else?

Porn actresses are sexy (well, to a guy they are). They do things ON CAMERA (oooh!) to men that most guys who obsess over porn will *never, e-v-e-r* have done to them. *THIS is why porn is so popular.* Guys see girls actually doing things they could never INSPIRE their wives, girlfriends, or mistresses to do. But all in all, it's just sex.

Marilyn Monroe, Sophia Loren, and Angelina Jolie are sexy; but unlike so many other actresses, <u>they have captured the hearts</u> of millions of men all over the world (in addition to their lust). They revel(ed) in their femininity and, through their stage personalities, allowed men to feel a bond with them, even though they never met. **They seduced the heart, not just the sex drive.**

AND SO
SHOULD
YOU!

As a woman, you were born with a certain quality called "femininity." Unfortunately, this quality, while still in high demand, has fallen from popularity, losing ground to one of its counterparts, "sex appeal." Sex appeal is overrated by mediocre minds (I won't mention exact names, but I am sure that you have met a few guys that fall into this category) and then these same inferior minds wonder why they are so dissatisfied with the women they date, who, in turn, are *deeply dissatisfied by them.* It's up to you to change all of this.

Here's how to do it:

<u>Your femininity consists of</u> your charm, sex appeal, nurturing ability, emotional makeup, physical beauty, and various other qualities you were born with. Your goal in life should be to exploit your strengths, while bringing up your weak parts so they are not detrimental to getting what you want—*when you want it.*

You influence men by the fact that you possess femininity naturally—because this is what we want more than money, power, and fame. *The very reason we break our backs and necks to get money, power, and fame <u>is to guarantee ourselves</u> that you will shower us with your complete femininity.*

We want your sex, attention, affection, your caring for us, loyalty, your children (at some point), your companionship . . . <u>When we are starved for attention</u> (and too many men are, especially in America), <u>all of our focus is on sex,</u> because we are hungry—and when you are hungry, all you can think about is food, and what it will take to get something to eat. But there is so much more!

As if we (guys) were not hungry enough, marketing experts know that we *will buy <u>anything</u>* if they simply promise us your affection and appreciation in exchange for trading our hard-earned cash for whatever they want to sell us.

This increases the pressure to keep buying things that will get us attention and sex. This is great for the economy, but bad for the heart. We end up wanting you sexually (even more than we would normally), and fail to realize that *we also need* emotional nurturing.

A better way to influence men, rather than allowing the onus to be placed entirely on sex, is to spend more time in places where sex is not possible, *but a certain level of intimacy is.* This is the basis of romance. Sharing experiences with a guy, and making those times enjoyable for both of you, is a much better way to sway him to your way of thinking rather than simply allowing him to set the pace and direction of your relationship by dragging you off to locations he has chosen to meet his needs.

Of course, you are not "delaying sex" to get more free stuff from the guy. You are simply rounding out your experiences with him. For example: Meeting him at the museum versus allowing him to cajole you into meeting him at the bar around 9 p.m.

<Ring>

Him:

blah, blah . . . "so when can we get together . . . blah, blah, blah . . ."

You:

"My week is really busy, but it would be nice to see you. Hey! I am going to be at the art museum on Sunday around noon. We can spend a few hours together then if you are available."

Him:

(thinking: Crap! I can't get laid at a museum!)

"Um . . . yeah, how about I meet you after the museum . . ."

You:

"That's the thing—I am supposed to meet Denise afterwards. Maybe we can get together another time. But if you change your mind, do you know where the museum is?"

Take a look at what you have done in this example:

"My week is really busy, but it would be nice to see you."

Right here, you have blamed circumstance on your lack of time. Then you have covered that by stating how it would please you to see him. This creates a psychological obligation on his part.

He has to recognize that you want to see him *(that's the part he likes)*, but outside forces are keeping you apart. Only a selfish jerk would blame you at this point.

"Hey! I am going to be at the art museum on Sunday around noon."

Well now . . . isn't that an interesting coincidence—9.9 times out of 10 the guy won't see how you set this up.

"We can spend a few hours together then if you are available."

Aren't you just the nicest girl ever? You are inviting him to come see you while you are doing something that normally you would reserve for your "personal time." Even if he declines, you have come across with a heartfelt invitation. If he passes that up, he can't say that you didn't try to see him.

"That's the thing—I am supposed to meet Denise afterwards."

Oh sure, blame the "friend" for hogging your time. But, you have already told him when you will be available—and asked him to come see you. Now you are simply in negotiations of when you two will meet.

"Maybe we can get together another time. But if you change your mind, I'd love to see you. Do you know where the museum is?"

Okay, so here you have gotten downright underhanded. He obviously has no desire to go to any museum with you, so instead of pressing the point (nagging him), or getting snide, you simply cut him off. BUT, you did it politely by saying that you can "get together some other time."

Then, as a continuation of that thought (<u>not</u> a pause and then a new thought; this part is very important), you told him that "if he changes his mind" (meaning that you respect his decision) . . . and then finished by asking him if he knows where the museum (which he has no interest in) is.

Remind me not to get into an argument with you! You have completely dominated the conversation, and forced him into a decision where he must either take the time with you <u>that is available</u> or do without seeing you. **You have not been a "bitch"** about it at all, so the only thing he can complain about is the amount of time "you have for him." You can use variations of this, endlessly, to get the men in your life to spend a good portion of their time with you when and wherever you want. The biggest risk you face is that they will look for someone who is more available.

This is just one example of how to easily plant a suggestion of implied romance in a guy's mind, even if you are already dating him. You are controlling his time with you <u>without making it look like you are trying to control him</u>. By the way, this is an excellent (and fast) way of ascertaining how a guy thinks of you, *what he will and won't do for you, and how manipulative <u>he</u> is.*

If, for example, he *does show up* at the museum but spends all of the time trying to get you to leave with him to go someplace else, you know what he wants, and how little he cares about "time with you." <u>Now you can decide what is best for you.</u> There are many ways to work on a guy's heart. Start by planning out your time with him in quasi-intimate settings that allow you to show him your femininity *instead of your breasts.* Use your breasts to close the deal if you feel so inclined.

How to bewitch a man
(just in case no one ever told you)

Note: The following items are not "pass or fail." You already possess each of them in varying degrees. You can build up or tear down any of them, at any time. Your goal should be to maximize the amount of each of your choices.

These tools of seduction are at your disposal, anytime you need them. Use them wisely and you will have guys drooling all over you as surely as if you fed them eye of newt potion, which I can get you (at a fair price) by the way . . .

*** *Be any 3 (or more)* <u>*below:*</u> ***

Pretty (to him). If you are going after a certain guy, find out what look he likes and be that, as much as you can without "changing yourself."

Charming. *Charm is all about personality.* There are millions of women who are considered "hot," but due to their personality flaws, and their attitudes, possess no charm or warmth whatsoever. Guys will have sex with them and end up "using them" *as punishment for being such "self-centered bitches."* Don't write me hate mail, I am just reporting the facts. <u>Men do NOT like</u> women who feel that their looks make them so superior to everyone else that the world must bend over and kiss their asses. The myth that men worth dating actually "love bitches" is just that: A *lie*.

Fun. To guys, "moderately pretty" girls who like to get out of the house and do things guys generally like are treated MUCH better (and actually listened to) than pretty girls who are high maintenance.

Friendly. Let's be clear about this: *"Friendly" does NOT mean "weak," easily manipulated, or "easy."* The fact that we live in an ever-increasingly selfish and isolationist society, where it is easier to ignore people than it is to be friendly and considerate (even to your friends), <u>makes it more powerful than ever</u> to be seen as friendly and "nice." You don't have to go out of your way to make people like you, *but if you can make them see you as a good person,* many of them will go out of their way for you.

Feminine. Most men will never learn from the countless mistakes of their forefathers. Properly applied femininity is THE CHIEF WEAKNESS of men everywhere and it makes them do incredibly stupid things <u>every day</u>, without fail. It is so dangerous to society that it should be *regulated*. Fortunately for you, it is not. Use it and "win."

"In need." See "Damsel in distress—Does that old ploy still work?" later in this book.

Affectionate (to him, and to your friends). Being nice and affectionate is NOT equivalent *to being servile*. Being affectionate (by gesture or action) is all about spreading your particular brand of sunshine, and nothing, including your looks, will make you more popular than that.

Loyal (to your friends, and your family, to him), but never in ways that go against your core belief system.

Seductive (in moderation—use as much as you think best).

Graceful (Klutzy is "cute," but grace clouds the mind quite nicely).

. . . and with that out of the way—it's time for . . .

Questions to ask yourself
before getting serious about ANY guy
(and every few months after you do . . .)

Between each extreme below is a middle ground—find yours.

How much do I want a guy in my life *right now*?	**How much time do I want with him throughout the week?** *(take a guess)*
I am not complete without one	Oh my god! Where is he right now? What is he doing?!!
I could use some companionship right now	Can't you leave me alone? I saw you yesterday!
The quality of this guy is:	**My interest level in this relationship is:**
He's worth so much more . . .	This is "the one"
Why am I here?	When's the next bus?
How happy am I right now?	**This guy makes me feel . . .**
"Wheee!!"	Like a goddess!
"Whaaa!"	Pretty bad (or worse)

Rule #4:

If a guy is <u>not cooperating</u>

(he is resisting your charm, pushing you too hard, or he is always trying to manipulate you),

DUMP HIM OFF!!

Why? Why? Why?

1: There are p-l-e-n-t-y of men **you will like** out there, and they are closer than you think. A lot of them are cute too. So why are you wasting your time *with this clown?* You could be in Aruba right now with a prince of a guy. *Well, you <u>could</u> be.* It's really up to you.

2: He would love to spend time with you "if only he knew your best parts" (so . . . it's time to show them!). I think I remember the Bible saying something about not hiding your light under a bushel of something or other. Well, I am not sure what a bushel is (maybe it's like a berka—and why would you want to hide under a berka?).

3: While you are out there kissing frogs looking for your prince(s), "Mr. Uncooperative" will either come to his senses or lose you (his loss, not yours—always remember that). **Either way, you win.**

4: **No man is as important as <u>the right man;</u>** and the right man would never ignore or pressure you unduly.

Think about that.

How to get your guy "friends" to give/buy you stuff!!

It all comes down to this . . .

What you are about to read is not fair. But, life is not "fair," so it is okay. The rules of friends, dating, and relationships were written long ago by a bunch of stuffy old codgers more intent on controlling the actions of future generations (er . . . that would be *you*) than they were with having fun. So the fact that guys everywhere will continue to waste *trillions of dollars a year* on women—just to impress them—is a sign of weakness on their part, and should not bother you. After all, if guys were giving away *free* money, you'd take that—right? **So let's think of anything a guy gives you (to impress you) as free money.** This means that you can save your money for more productive uses. *That's just smart financial management!*

Your male "friends" consist of various categories: guys who like your personality, want to have sex with you, or have a crush on you but can't seem to find the right way to tell you without risking chasing you away. Big deal. So a guy "wants" you. Take that as a compliment.

If you have *anything* (at all) going for you—looks, personality, charm—you will have more than a few of these guys in your life at all times. The fact that they are your "friends" means that they *like you* and will subvert their own desires to bring you a little happiness in life. They are great to practice your "getting guys to do what you want" skills on. **After all, they are going to spend money on girls no matter what *you* do.** From there to having guys buying you diamonds at Tiffany's is but a small step.

Here's how to get there:

There is a certain etiquette to follow when a guy gives you a gift unexpectedly. Follow this etiquette in every situation, and you will easily train the men you meet to eventually start buying you things. Of course, some guys will be easier to train than others, but then who doesn't like a fun challenge? You personally may know this etiquette, but it is obvious, simply by looking around, that most people do not. So, with that in mind, here is the etiquette of receiving gifts of any size.

Act mildly surprised. Over time it should become commonplace for men to give you things, take you on trips, pay for your meals, entertainment, and yes, even sex (by giving you nicer and nicer gifts). Isn't this the exploitation of women? Of course not. Perish the thought. It is simply men being stupid.

A guy will easily waste tens of thousands of dollars or more (directly and indriectly) every year on women, hoping to impress them enough to take an interest in him. In fact, far too many guys you meet will expect that a girl will be impressed *simply by the dollar amount spent on her.* These guys refuse to <u>invest that money in themselves</u> to learn not to be such an idiot around women (through seminars, makeovers, and perhaps picking up a passion for life), because their egos will not allow them to admit that they are not complete studs. The most self-improvement the average guy will undergo is to go to the gym to "beef up" a bit.

Any man who thinks that it is a better idea to throw his money at you in a desperate attempt to impress you (into bed), *rather than work on himself to become more attractive to you,* deserves for you to take his money and say "thank you!"

Be appreciative!!

The size of the gift does not matter. **It is the very act of giving that you are recognizing, and enticing more of from him.** It is easy to *think* of doing something nice for someone. Actually *doing* something nice for someone requires effort. We are encouraging *action.*

<u>The gift you get today is the gateway to bigger gifts and a bright future</u>. A sincere *"thank you,"* along with one of your devastating smiles, that you will soon be practicing, will lodge itself in a guy's mind, and be the beginning of an addiction to please you, if you nurture that addiction. Positive reinforcement will train the guy to make you happy. Successfully done, this will, in turn, make him happy. And making a guy happy (for making you happy) is a really good feeling to have.

. . . and oops! Was that your hand that landed on his shoulder accidentally as you said "thank you," but was gone before he had time to fully notice? Wow, suddenly he seems to be thinking of you quite often. The slightest actions and personality traits (see *My major hooks*) you combine with your showing of appreciation *"for him"* (not just for the presents he gives you) will enslave a man to you. By showing simple, sincere appreciation for the thought (first), the gift (second), and for him being such a considerate friend (third and fourth), you are subtly training your male "friend(s)" to *buy/give you things without even thinking about it.*

Think about it this way: We all love seeing the light in a child's eye on Christmas when they open their presents. <u>Why would you even think of denying your</u> (male) <u>friends that kind of joy</u>? What kind of "friend" would you be anyway, if you denied your friends the chance to make themselves a bit happier for a few moments?

Share with your friends *"the Magic of Christmas"* all year long by getting a twinkle in your eye whenever they buy you lunch, or give you a gift, a trip, new Mercedes . . . Just don't be too over the top with your appreciation. Not that they would generally mind, but it does circumvent the whole point of training them to give freely, and often. Every little trinket is a token of his desire to please you. Wouldn't it be nice if every man you met was overwhelmed with a desire to please you?

Return the favor. This means when a friend gives you something, give them something back. Don't be too obvious here. If a guy buys you lunch, buy him a (non-romantic) gift that you think he would enjoy, but wait a few days. This means doing a little research, but if you do this properly, and often, you will *own* the guys in your life.

If, for example, your friend likes golf and he is the "serious type," stop by a pro golf shop and get him some expensive balls (just a small box). Wrap them up creatively and casually give him the gift at a time and place of your choosing (when he is not preoccupied), and say that you "saw these in your travels" (be mysterious) and you thought of him. (Lie and) tell him that the guy who sold them to you said that they were guaranteed to improve his game. If you are really good friends, tell him that you like a man with balls, and laugh. Don't linger too long lest he start thinking romantic thoughts. Let him surprise you with your next gift.

Your intention is to <u>establish a pattern</u> of escalating gift exchanges. He buys you something. You "just so happen" to bring in a home-made picnic basket one day at work and feed a few of your friends (including him of course). Or, he buys you lunch, and you spy a trinket. Eventually he should be offering you trips (which you may choose to accept or reject based on your feelings toward him—but when he has gone that far, you have done well).

Size up your male friends and see which one(s) you think will be happy to "share their friendship with you" (give freely), and which ones you think would be more stingy. Begin by lavishing your generous friends with casual compliments, and occasional casual hints like, "Oh . . . I saw _____ at the store the other day and for some reason I thought of you. I almost picked it up for you but I didn't know if you would like something like that." Find out if you are good at guessing what they like.

Plant the suggestion <u>casually</u> in their heads that you wouldn't waste time thinking twice on whether or not you *should* pick up a little ($10–$30) trinket you saw if you thought it was perfect for them. Surprise them on occasion with inexpensive ($3–$8) knickknacks for no special reason—if you can find something that really matches them, their style, or makes them laugh (perhaps an inside joke you two have). Any "real man" will try to outdo your amateurish attempt at gift giving. A "real man" will spend 2–5 times more than you because his ego demands it. Hopefully, you have chosen a lot of "real men" as friends.

It is best to be a bit preemptive with this strategy (you go first). Pick a few friends and start their training, measuring your progress. Try "picking up the tab" at lunch on one of your better marks (he is nice, AND makes a good amount of money . . .) when you know that it won't be too much for you to handle comfortably.

Whatever you do, do NOT say, "Oh, you'll get it next time."

If he says something to that effect, act mildly surprised and say "Thank you! . . . but please don't worry about it. I enjoyed the company," or something like that which doesn't emasculate him, seem like you're ignoring his offer, or comes across as sappy and romantic. Then start planning a trip to your favorite moderately expensive bistro where he will end up "picking up the tab."

Your investment should primarily be charm, appreciation (of him, as a person), thoughtfulness, and, of course, a few minutes to carefully select the right present. His reciprocation should be buying you larger and larger gifts in return. This will take some practice. This will also come easier to some of you than it will to others. The deciding factors will be your smile (you have been practicing—*right?*), your sincerity, appreciation, generosity, and your selection of men.

Ask. Do it playfully, but don't be afraid to ask for stuff. You will be surprised at how often you get stuff (free). Start with small, inconsequential things until you build up your asking skills and confidence. Practice on your best friends. Be sure to return the favor by doing things for them that make them feel as if you are a very good friend, but in reality didn't cost you a lot of money.

Make the guy feel good for being kind. Make him feel like a man. Everyone likes to feel good about themselves, and every man likes to feel like more of a man, when he can. *Everything above adds up to this one point.* Just make your men feel special for being so kind, and they will try to replicate (or outdo) that feeling time and time again. Pavlov wasn't so silly after all.

Quick! I need $40 for a pair of shoes
(or lunch, a flat tire, tip for the valet . . .)

. . . so you hit the ATM and the stupid machine says that you have no money. Machines are stupid. They are always eating my money somehow. If you are running a little low on cash, and payday is still a few days away, let me remind you of the amazing benefits of having guy "friends." Hit one up for a few 20's and fix him dinner later in the week as a thank you. Bring it over to his place along with an action flick and make sure to talk through the movie (like you do at Rocky Horror). Have fun and make it a great night. It helps you get through a tough week, and have a fun night with a guy, *not being pressured.* And isn't that what friendship is all about anyway?

In a guy's mind . . .
The perfect girlfriend

Age 15	Age 21
Girl shows up, with latest X-Box game, in BMW her daddy bought her (but she let's you drive). Gets her braces off next week, likes to kiss, and allows you to feel her up sometimes.	Models for a living, but has a job at the library because she hates the idea of "getting paid for her looks." Buys the beer occasionally. Doesn't flirt with your friends, but she loves to do "guy stuff" with you (hiking, touch football, snowboarding, etc.). She's low maintenance, dresses casual but can make you drool when she puts on a dress. Brings over her girlfriend once in a while for sex. Non-pressuring.
Age 30	**Age 50+**
Younger than you are. Physically a "7" or better. *Great personality:* laid-back, fun. Hopefully has a few lingering traits from Age 21 fantasy girl. Gives you affection without you having to ask for it. Brings beer, or goes shopping when the game is on, doesn't nag you, and of course, she allows you to complain about how your wife just doesn't *understand you* anymore.	Still likes sex occasionally. Is attracted to you (at all), and you are attracted to her. Knows a few kinky tricks to surprise you with every once in a while.

78

PRACTICE
your smile!

What happens to a man when you smile at him?

<u>In a friendly way</u>: His attitude toward you softens, he feels warm inside, and a swelling of energy fills his chest. He feels good about himself and good about you. This makes him open to suggestion. If the guy already likes you, this one smile is likely to cause him to do several stupid things (most of which you will probably not see, but would get a good laugh out of if you did).

<u>In a sweet, almost shy way</u>: WARNING! Do not use this smile lightly. If overused, this smile may turn against you (the guy may catch on, and in the case of stupid and/or uncultured men, this can be bad). <u>Save it for special occasions</u>.

The power of this smile, delivered properly, can decimate armies of men. Your "sweet smile," if it is believable, will *effortlessly* toss aside all logic in a guy's mind, and utterly destroy all resistance on its way to his heart. Once there, it will tug at it with the soft gentleness of a summer breeze—backed by the power of an avalanche. The dichotomy of this will make his head snap back and forth (which is fun to watch) as his heart grows to enormous size, overpowering all other bodily functions. You will tap into his protective nature and his secret weakness to feminine innocence that runs through even the most hardened of men.

If you do this successfully *(all you have to do is practice)*, you will have his unwavering loyalty at that instant, and the image of your smile will burn itself into his consciousness forever. Choose your next words carefully. At this moment, very few men on earth could resist your command (depending on how adept you have become) if you have chosen the right time and place to hit him with your perfect delivery of this smile.

<u>With your seductive smile</u>: Another one not to be taken lightly. Bandy this one around and you will earn a reputation, and it will lose its effect entirely, except on cretins (*and who wants to date those?*).

Of all smiles to practice, this one is paramount. Application of this smile allows for no failure. If you deliver this smile poorly, you will at the least turn the man off, possibly sicken him to the very thought of you, or even repulse him outright. His attitude will harden to stone, and you will find it extremely difficult to ever entice him again.

The best person to practice this smile on is your boyfriend (get one, even a disposable one, and perfect it on him). You need to look your best (or close to it) when you toss this smile out, and your timing will have to be pretty good as well. This smile is rather high maintenance (as far as smiles go). It requires full commitment. It is far better to commit fully to this smile, and break into laughter, than it is to try to do this halfway.

Smile with your entire body. Start with your eyes, <u>*filling your mind and heart with intoxication for him*</u>. Feel that energy spreading throughout your body and use that to fuel your own seductiveness. Allow that wave of energy to seep into every fiber of your being. Hold an image in your mind of writhing erotically to a sensual beat to add to the effect. Don't worry; no one can see inside your head to see what you are thinking. The more you can raise the level of your passion, your sacred inner fire, the more naturally your body will respond to your call.

Once you have mastered this smile, you will be able to hit a man with it without much thought at all, and he will not be able to forget you. <u>He will punch through mountains with his bare fists to reach you</u>, swim oceans to be near you, cure diseases to impress you, and (regrettably) leave other women to have you. You will make other women *insanely jealous* at your power over (their) men. The power of this smile will make a man your willing slave (er . . . "protector") if you desire. Perfect it completely, use it wisely, and rarely.

Of course, after you have developed your ability to plant this smile on a man even a little, you can toss out miniature versions of this smile *through your eyes* at will. Have fun toying with men in a non-committal way, the way a cat toys with a mouse it has by the tail. Use it to melt men's hearts—and keep yours in line.

With your innocent smile: This is a far less dramatic variation of the shy/sweet smile, and so you can use it as often as you like on men. It works best on strangers, often getting them to do "nice things for you" without having to ask, and is a great way to say thank you for a guy doing a small favor like holding the door open for you. You can never get too much practice, and the effect will have men you meet everywhere thinking kind thoughts of you. The next time they see you, they will have a preconceived notion of you as a "good person," one they want to help out, protect, or become friends with.

You should know that this smile will have a completely different effect on the self-proclaimed "pimps" and "players" you bump into occasionally. These guys will almost always see through this smile immediately and they will invariably try to get you under their influence (and then control) as fast as possible, so that they can profit from your use of this smile on other men. This makes this smile a great "asshole detector," as men are unbelievably predictable when you start to understand them *(keep reading, keep practicing)*.

With an insincere smile: This mockery of social grace is a slap in the face to anyone you bestow it upon. Best used on your nemesis, and never in public (where you can be caught using it).

fun facts!

As a rule, women paint their nails, do their hair in an infinite variety of styles, wear makeup, padded bras, stockings, sexy dresses, and go to the gym, all in the name of beauty; but they don't want men to *want them for their looks*.

Conversely, men (as a rule) ignore the gym, allow themselves to get fat *and* bald, wear the same clothes e-v-e-r-y day (a "suit"), and do everything they can (legal or not) **to make more money to be more attractive to women** and then *complain that women only want them for their money*.

Who made these crazy rules for society anyway?

How to blow off a guy
without him feeling rejected
and telling all of his friends what a bitch you are
(to soothe his damaged ego)

Okay, so the two of you have been talking for a few minutes and you want to leave—or he asks for your phone number and you don't want him calling you. Forget the "I have a boyfriend" or "I am really flattered" lines. Guys have heard these so many times they will either have a comeback or they will lump you in with "all the other girls who used that line on them." Try these instead, or make up your own!

"I'm in the process of moving. Can I get your number?"

"Maybe next time we meet."

"Tell you what—here's my email address. I don't get a chance to check it every day, but if you write, I will definitely read it." (Have a "free email" address that you save for just such an occasion.)

If you absolutely can't leave, fake a stomach cramp, quietly say "diarrhea" and head for the bathroom. Excuse yourself while you get some more coffee (spill yours if you have to), or chew off your arm like a coyote caught in a bear trap.

Ask him what time it is. Apologize and make a call right in front of him. Call a friend and apologize to her for being late for/missing her son's bar mitzvah. You can explain to her later—besides, she probably could use a good laugh at your expense anyway.

Speaking of which . . .

How to dump a guy
so that he will stay dumped!

Don'tcha hate it when you dump someone and they are so amazed at how great you are that they keep calling, and calling? Your email inbox is stuffed with messages from them, and even your "letter carrier" (mailman) is complaining about the weight of all of the apology cards you get every day. On days like this, I wonder why I even bother dating. Well, the best way to get someone to "go away," when it is truly over, is to <u>make them lose interest in you</u>. Here's one of the easier ways:

Lose interest in him. This means *you don't care* what he thinks of you. Stop dressing sexy around him if you can. Stop wearing make-up and perfume. The more unattractive you are to him, the faster he will run into some other girl's arms. Frown a lot around him. Don't scowl at him. Simply appear generally unhappy, uptight, and bored (all of the time) whenever he is in the area. This may be too much effort, so feel free to use sparingly. Practice your complaining skills on him. Be flaky, disinterested in him, and if you must talk to him, be sure to maneuver the conversation toward subjects that he has no interest in.

Making him go away
(buhbye now)

Sometimes you find yourself in a situation where a guy just won't stop bothering you. You would be fine if he would just leave you alone. Here are a few fun suggestions for ridding yourself of unwanted pests whether:

1: You just met

2: You don't want to "just meet"

3: He won't stop calling you

4: It's time for a divorce

. . . Of course you could always just say "Go Away!" to a guy who is so enamored with you that he just can't seem to control himself. But really, how often does *that* work? Besides, he might take it the wrong way and get angry. Then he has to salvage his ego, especially if he thinks any of his friends saw you blow him off. So, just for fun, let's consider what you might do if:

1: <u>You just met</u>—and he turns out to be a jerk, complete loser, clinging vine, bully, etc.

If you just met a guy and you need to lose him fast, but you don't want an argument, try yawning. Then apologize. Don't worry about being polite (that means not covering your mouth). After all, you DO want him to go away and not ever come back, right? Tell him that you didn't get much sleep last night.

Don't make any overt attempts to leave just yet (as <u>he might follow you</u>; after all, you *are* heading to bed . . .). Excuse yourself and go to the bathroom for a few minutes. We hate waiting for you while you are in the bathroom. We feel stupid. We get impatient. We look at other girls and wonder if we can score with them tonight.

So you are hanging out in the bathroom, doing whatever it is that you do, for a few minutes, giving him the chance to "do the right thing" (like bother some other girl—or leave), but even if he doesn't, *it sends a clear message.*

It also gives you a few moments to think, or call a friend without him drooling all over you.

You could spill your drink . . .

. . . on the table, floor, him—*does it really matter?* Apologize, quickly jump up and run for a waiter, the door . . . Refuse to allow him to buy you another drink.

Drop your cell phone (gently of course—or better yet, have an old one in your purse for just such an emergency). Then pick it up and

"test it" (in front of him of course). If it works, call a friend—where you find out that your friend has been trying to call you—and they have a minor (believable) emergency that you have to attend to *RIGHT NOW.* Apologize and *scram!*

Start ranting about women's issues, or just disagree with anything he says that you feel you can hold your own on . . .

2: You don't want to "just meet"

Uh oh . . . that creepy guy is making eyes at you. He looks like he is on his way over. Where are your stupid "friends" when you NEED them (like now)! Great! Here he comes . . . Pull out your cell phone and make a call. Just hit redial and talk to whoever answers. Most guys have an aversion to a girl yakking on her cell phone. This trick will ward off all but the dumbest, and most obnoxious, jerks.

3: He won't stop calling you

Before you change your phone number, try having some of your friends answer your phone. Sometimes they can answer as if it is now their phone (*the cover story is that they inherited your old phone*). Other times they can say that you stepped away and that they answered it thinking your new boyfriend was calling, or they can try to pick up on him (especially if they are guys).

It's really fun if your friends speak another language and they simply answer the phone in a language he doesn't understand—and then start yelling at him, telling him to "get his chicken out of their front yard before they make soup out of it."

Have fun handing the phone to strangers whenever your caller ID shows him calling. Just ask them to say hello and to act confused when he asks for you, as if they never heard of anyone having that name. If one of your guy "friends" is around, have him answer it in a low voice and say, "No, she's in the shower at the moment" and hang up. It may not get him to stop calling right away, but it is hours of endless fun, and he can't blame you for the phone company screwing up his calls.

If you don't have caller ID, or he calls you from another number, have a prearranged signal with your friend (preferably one he doesn't know) that you can flash the moment you say hello and he starts talking. Your friend can start yelling, "Hey! Give me back my phone!" and then have a pretend argument with your friend about whose phone it really is, and how you were using it to make a call when he called, and why is he calling your friend anyway (he can overhear all of this), and then hang up and laugh, and laugh. When he calls back (in a few seconds), let the phone ring a few times and have your friend answer the phone angrily—and when he/she finds out the call is for you, your friend pretends to yell at you about giving out their number. Hang up again and stop answering the phone for half an hour. Laugh at how confused he should be by now. Then have some fun arguing with your friend over who is the better actress/actor.

The most fun part of playing these reindeer games with your best friends (and the occasional stranger) answering your phone whenever he calls is that it gives the impression to this jerk that you are constantly surrounded by tons of friends. *You are super popular!* Unless the guy is a total stalker (in which case you seriously need to call the police—that's what they are for), hopefully, the image of you being so popular will be depressing and demotivational and he'll just *leave you alone*. But just in case: There are detailed "Help Pages" at the very end of this book if you ever get caught up in any seriously bad situations and need some help getting out safely.

In the average man's mind, every male "friend" he knows you have really means there are 2–3 others that he knows nothing about. Suddenly he is imagining you surrounded by men everywhere you go. This alone can drive a man away, or drive him insane. If you suspect the guy IS a stalker type, call the police and be done with him.

Of course, *don't tell the guy that you are going to call the police.* Don't you watch horror movies? You know that never works—yet far too many women *still* make this mistake. Why? Why? Why? Don't answer that. Just don't make the same mistake.

4: It's time for a divorce

Okay—so you are in a relationship and you just want him to go away, but you don't want to be "the bad guy." Unless you are involved with a jealous and/or violent idiot, try being unavailable. Guys really hate that. Work more hours (the money is good—and think of all the fun stuff you will be able to buy once "he" is gone), volunteer time for local charities, get a second job, or take a few classes at a local college. Space and unavailability create emotional distance. By making "circumstance" the culprit, you remove any possible blame from yourself. This creates a solid foundation for separation. It also starts the process of developing habits associated with not seeing each other. This, in itself, makes the eventual "permanent separation" that much easier.

How to turn a guy who really likes you into "a friend," *gently and easily*

Oh sure . . . give me an easy one . . . Well, pour yourself a nice hot cup of your favorite coffee, because this one will be very delicate, and you will need to have your wits about you. <u>What we are attempting to do is</u> lower his burning flame for you from BOIL to SIMMER. If you try to toss water onto his fire, you will just end up spattering grease everywhere.

So, you like this guy. You really *like* him. He's funny, nice, supportive, caring, and would probably make a great father one day; but the thought of kissing him makes your skin crawl. He's the perfect "friend" except for one small detail. You know he wants you. What's a girl to do? Here are a few surefire techniques to taming his fire, and turning him into a loyal, lifelong friend. Kinda like a brother. *You have to catch this early,* preferably when you have an idea how he feels, but he hasn't yet made it completely obvious. The longer you let his infatuation with you go on, the harder it will be to turn him into a reliable friend. You need to make sure that your time with him is not intimate. If you two *are* alone, <u>make sure there are no sunsets conveniently nearby</u>, and your eyes should not "glisten green with a hint of moonlight upon the angry seas." Obviously you want to be wary of romantic overtones in the beginning. Whenever you can, get together with your friend around much prettier girls/women, or conversely, hang out with "the guys." It's hard for a guy to hit on you in front of his buddies, especially if they have accepted you as "one of the guys." Of course, it always helps if you dress down a bit to enhance the effect.

Coffeehouses are a great place to meet up with your male friends early on in your friendship. The balance of *implied intimacy in public* (other people will generally not be listening in on your conversation even though they are sitting three feet away), *with the obvious lack of any romantic intimacy*, will help establish the ideal settings to build a "friendship." It is also convenient how easily one of your (female) friends can drop by. Pepper your conversations occasionally with topics that will turn him off to you a little, just to make sure that you don't always end up talking about issues that will endear him to you even more.

If you can, hook him up with someone—anyone. Set him up on a date! Be his "wing girl" (go out with him to clubs and other places and tell the women you meet how great he is). Help him get dates. Then do it again if that doesn't work out. Setting your friend(s) up with dates not only makes guys like (and appreciate) you, but it sends a strong message that is pretty clear—to all but the most "desperately in love with you"—that you are *"just friends"* without having to hammer it home to him. It is also a much more positive way of getting the message across.

When you meet him, especially the first dozen times, try to meet when you are with an attractive and friendly female friend of yours. If she blows him off mercilessly, repeat this with another, and another (attractive) female friend. Trust me, the guy will never catch on. Not if he has a pulse. Dress down whenever you get together. Have clothes on hand that make you look dumpy, or plain, and change into them when he comes over, or you two go out. Sure you are risking not looking your best when "Mr. Right" comes along, but "Mr. Right" would see through your "dressing down" disguise anyway, and think you all the more a goddess.

Are you a <u>germaphobe</u>?

Take this fun quiz and find out!

"Ewww!! That's Gross!"

"You want me to put that <u>where</u>?"

(Score one point for each "yes!")

1. Do you carry a toothbrush and toothpaste with you everywhere you go? What about mouthwash?

2. How many times a day do you wash your hands? Do you use <u>soap</u>? *(Score one point for each time you wash your hands on average in your regular day.)*

3. Do you use either hand sanitizer or antibacterial soap?

4. Do you have ANY idea just how many guys you meet every day <u>don't</u> *wash their hands* at all after they use the bathroom at work? *(Especially "busy" <u>executives!</u>)*

5. How often do men <u>touch</u> or shake hands with <u>you</u> every day?

6. Are you aware that you can get an STD simply from *touching* an "adult DVD"?*

7. Did you know that you can get salmonella just by *smelling* raw chicken?*

8. Did you hear about that science experiment where the girl found all of that bacteria in restaurant ice? Not to worry though, I hear that bacteria can't grow in cold temperatures.

   <u>Congratulations</u>! If you weren't a germaphobe a moment ago, **you probably are now.**

  (*urban myths)

How to steal a man
("Oops!")

(*not recommended . . . but if you must . . .*)

Stolen men generally have a way of turning out not worth stealing, or simply going sour on you over time. If you absolutely must have that cute guy some other bitch is neglecting but won't let go of, and you are sure that this guy is not just a player working your emotions into a frenzy (or you just don't care), there are some basic rules to follow. Yes, even stealing has rules.

1: Be subtle! The operative term here is "plausible deniability." Simply put, that means that you can feign innocence when you are accused of trying to steal "her" man. Leave no evidence. I won't tell you how to do this.

2: Be obvious! Lipstick marks on a man's collar have ended more relationships over the generations than any man actually ever being caught in bed with another woman. The *implication* of infidelity has a way of killing off intimacy immediately (so much for "innocent until proven guilty"), and from there it is a short trip to the strip clubs in the time-honored pilgrimage guys make in search of subtle emotional validation from interacting with a naked woman.

Panties *(not yours of course!)* under the passenger seat of his car will start fights you can hear from a few blocks away (you bring the popcorn, I'll bring the beer and lawn chairs). Unfortunately they can be equally devastating to wives, girlfriends, and kids, so *at least try* to be careful not to hurt others on your path to stealing your preferred man. Karma aside, it is just in bad taste.

<u>To be blunt</u>: Arouse suspicion of him, in "her." Know that *if you do this and you are caught,* you will most likely end up losing—and I <u>don't</u> mean bad karma. I mean that you are opening yourself up to potential violence or slander. So if you absolutely must do this, don't tell anyone what you are up to.

3: Be better than she is. Cook, clean (your place of course, not his), dress "pretty but sexy," flirt lightly, and most of all, <u>live with a true passion for life</u>. This is your most powerful tool for attracting the very best men (and unfortunately some of the worst).

Be passionate about something and let the world see it. Nothing inspires lust and longing in a potential partner (and hate/jealousy in your potential adversaries) like a sincere passion for life.

Don't fake it. Take advantage of the fact that so few women who meet the same men have so little passion for life. Turn off your television once a week and pursue a cause. Be artistic, athletic, poetic, an activist; find causes or activities you naturally gravitate to and immerse yourself in them. When you live your life, actively chasing down your dreams, you unleash the very sexiest parts of your personality. The very best men will seek you out, while the "below average" slobs will be intimidated by you (which is nice, as it makes more room for the men you actually want to share your time with).

4: Be available where she is not. This is the number one way to steal a man—any man. The reason the stereotype evolved of executives having affairs with their secretaries is because the men had constant, close interaction with their assistants. Hmmm . . . let's review *that* scenario and see if we can decipher how a man might become enamored with a woman who is in close proximity to him on a daily basis, whether *she* has any interest in *him* or not.

Well, *she is* around him e-v-e-r-y day. Close, productive, repetitious encounters with a woman will build camaraderie (friendship which is always nice), arousal (a "must have" for any affair), and longing (the seeds of a relationship) in a man, especially an ambitious one (executive)—*especially if she is:*

Supportive: As his "administrative assistant" (call her what you will), she traditionally brings him coffee (just like mom, or his wife—how nice of her), so she is a nurturer. She also listens to his tirades and knows the best times to speak her mind, *and when not to.* Granted, she has little choice in the matter, but the fact is that **the most powerful** secretaries throughout time have known exactly how and when to drop a suggestion here and there, which has, in turn, altered history *on their whims alone.* That is feminine empowerment at its finest: all of the power, and none of the blame if things go wrong. Whoever coined the phrase "True power lies *behind* the throne," must have been a secretary.

Helpful: All of her daily tasks *(the ones she is paid to do)* **add up over time** to give her the appearance to him as being "helpful" *in a partnership way;* which, over time, can become an extremely deep bonding experience. Imagine the closest two members of a team. An executive and his confidante, his assistant, his teammate who "has his back" at all times. She regulates who has access to him and keeps him on his schedule, so that he can focus on the tasks at hand. She makes him far more productive, which keeps them both employed. This makes him dependent on her to know her job *and even some of his.* They both work incredibly long hours (together), and they share the same knowledge. You would be amazed at how much your husband's secretary knows. Are you afraid of her yet? You should be.

(I have to get one of these "secretaries"!)

Her "boss's" mind does not make the distinction that this is merely a job to her. He subconsciously starts painting her in a light of beneficence, as if she is some form of a minor **saint.** Of course, this is not always the case *(some bosses are idiots),* but if you understand how and why office romances between executives and their secretaries flourish, then you will understand why men fall in love with their "administrative assistants."

94

These women have not sacrificed power. They have perfected the art of femininity—and *feminine influence*. Auntie Venus would be proud. They can get the most powerful men in the world to do things no other man or woman could ever hope to. **Like it or not:** The best secretaries in the world, *run the world.*

Loyal: A strange symbiosis often evolves in a successful working relationship between a secretary and her "executive" (her dependent). Her ability to stop anyone from being able to see or talk to him, or conversely, her ability to force him to stop what he is doing to interact with someone (an important client, or *his* boss), and her knowledge of his affairs, creates a closeness on a level that only his wife can reach him on. This is the basis for many an affair in and of itself. Having a woman truly understand and care for him is a goal most men share, but too few ever get.

Mysterious: All too often, the bond that forms over time between a secretary and her executive causes him to wonder *what she is like away from work.* She is an integral part of his work experience (which for men invariatably defines their identity in life) and then she simply disappears every night at five o'clock.

It is natural when working so closely with someone over a period of several years to ask about their personal life, to share intimate details of your own. But no matter how much he asks about this woman he seems to know so well, she always disappears like a genie every evening and weekends. In some cases this can create a fascination. In others, the executive could care less.

These and other factors can build a dependency in an executive for his assistant/confidante/junior partner/surrogate girlfriend. And then there are men who simply aspire to positions that "require" an assistant of some kind or another because they think this will be an easy way to obtain mistresses.

I have always marveled at how the word secretaries breaks down to: Secret Aries . . . How many times have you been frustrated by an "administrative assistant's" ability to stop you from being able to speak to an executive. A good secretary can stop bullets (well, she can make the world's most "powerful men" sit and wait *while she decides when and how to let them speak to her "boss"*).

Well, that was loads of fun. Please understand that this is just a quick examination of the absolute power professional secretaries can wield, should they choose to. This is not an indictment of their character, or of an executive's weaknesses. That must be taken on a case-by-case basis. For the most part, I am certain that secretaries have no idea at all how much influence they wield on a daily basis over the world's corporate affairs. Being that the world is becoming more of a corporate structure every day, one day these women will rule us all. I hope they will still make coffee.

(But back to this stealing thing again . . .)

5: Be unavailable if she is clingy (*once you have him hooked*). Don't send him signals of disinterest. Send him signals of your freedom, and how you live life as an adventure. Subtlety works well here. Mementos or casual hints about your adventures while he was "trapped at home" will dig under his skin like a splinter, where it will fester. It won't be long at all before he is complaining to you about how he longs for the life you live (hint: *with you* "Miss Free Spirit"). He will be living vicariously (and jealously) through your experiences—wishing he was there with you. Oh boo hoo. The idiot made his own bed—let him lie in it (with her). That should be enough to chase him into your web of seduction.

Your chosen man will start confiding all of his annoyances with "her"—with just a little prodding from you. If he starts this on his own, take it as a clear sign that he is attempting to lay the foundation for your eventual seduction. I am not sure why men complain about *their* woman *to other* women in the hopes of eliciting sympathy sex from them. Even I have done this in the distant past—and I still don't understand why. It just instinctively felt "like it should obviously work." Hmmm . . .

Alcohol (in him) works wonders to loosen the tongue, but keep the doses *small*. As obvious as this may seem, too many of you make the mistake of allowing too much alcohol to flow and trouble ensues. If you are on a mission to steal a man, do not lose focus of your objective. Having sex with him does not make him yours. Getting him to the point of abandoning everything in his life for you does.

Find out how distant (or clingy) she is and be her polar opposite, but be subtle, and never become something that you are not. Not for "him"; not for anyone. This is another seemingly obvious point that is ignored by men and women constantly—and reading this will not stop you from doing it as well. But I am feeling a bit ornery, so I will rant a bit:

You are "you." <u>Let me rephrase that in the language of your planet</u>: You are "you." **You always have been.** Before anyone taught you how to express yourself more coherently (speak, write, throw very convincing tantrums in public . . .), **you knew what you liked, and what you didn't.** Life is nothing more than a series of experiences that refine and shape who you are. All of these experiences are merely food for the soul. It is like a never-ending buffet of good food, bad food, exotic foods, and usually far too much run-of-the-mill food.

Eat healthy and you will generally have a very happy life. This means *surrounding yourself with quality people who care about you;* not selfish, narcissistic, drama-obsessed miscreants who suck the nutritional value of your experiences from your life. <u>This is why I spent so much time in Sections 1 and 2 reminding you to choose men who are good for you.</u> Find your passions and enjoy them with people who share those same passions in a supportive mindset. Happiness: Simple, easy, *and relatively instant.*

"Easier said than done!"

. . . I hear someone shouting from across the room as you read my self-righteous preaching aloud to a stunned, and disbelieving crowd . . . I freely admit that this is no easy task. <u>But neither is wasting your life on people who are so beneath you that they make the gum stuck to your shoe seem downright angelic.</u> Happiness is a matter of choice. Finding your passions and then surrounding yourself with the toys and tools necessary to experience those passions on a daily basis is a necessary step away from a blah, boring life.

What does *any of this* have to do with stealing a man from an unappreciative bitch who is obviously wasting his life? Well, if he truly would be happier with you *(and you with him—and that is what we are really after, isn't it?),* then there is a step along the way to surrounding yourself with your passions.

97

The "right man" adds much more to your life than just his presence (although we do like to think that our presence alone should be enough to make you happy). "Mr. Even-close-to-right" naturally inspires you, helps you feel better than you ever could without him (or else why do you need him anyway?) which, in turn, brings out some of the very best parts of you. It's all a giant snowball.

Okay, one last point on stealing men, and then I have had enough on this nefarious topic.

6: Be supportive, but challenging. Finding the balance between being supportive of his needs without being coddling and challenging enough to lead him *(yes, I said "lead him," but don't tell anyone I did)* to great heights—<u>without being perceived</u> (by him) <u>as a commanding or demeaning bitch</u>—is not easy. But if he is worth the effort of stealing (and the consequences thereof), then you will find a way. History has more than a few examples (hundreds of thousands come to mind at the moment) of women building their men up in such a way that their man was a true partner. Of course, the man got the glory, but that's the fun part about being a guy. Only the most "intellectually challenged" of us men <u>actually believe</u> that we truly are the ones in power. We are puppets, *but as long as we get to play with swords on stage, then we usually don't mind.*

That's about as much patience as I can muster for dishonesty. Good luck if you take this path. If not, then use these techniques to spot someone trying to steal your man.

How to tell the quality of a guy _instantly_ by giving him a present

Everyone loves presents. That's why Santa is such a popular guy. The trick in giving presents is knowing what presents to give to whom. You could spend your entire paycheck trying to impress your boss by buying him an expensive set of golf clubs, only to find out that he secretly hates the game and only plays it to impress _his_ boss. Or . . . you could spend twelve bucks on Amazon.com for a book on "how to be a hit at the 19th hole"* and get a nice Christmas bonus this year. The same rule applies to any guy.

*_Just so you know_ . . . Golf courses have either 9 or 18 holes. Don't ask me why—I despise the game personally. The "19th hole" is a colloquialism for the bar at the country club, where deals are made, contracts are signed, and who knows what else goes on. By giving your boss a book on "how to be a hit at the 19th hole," you help him look good _to his boss_. Hopefully, the selfish bastard will remember _your career_ and give you a raise.

Some guys get presents from girls all the time. But how do you know which ones score points for you, which ones make the guy think you are "some weird obsessive/possessive girl," and which ones are just a complete waste of money? You need:

"Mister X's" ~~Dusty's~~ Guide to Smart Gift Giving!

You can tell a lot about a guy, and how he feels about you—_instantly_—simply by giving him a gift. Start by choosing a gift around $10–$20 that you think closely fits his personality. Think "trinket," not _gloves, socks, or anything he could actually use_. By the way, this trick works equally well on guys you have just met, as well as husbands, boyfriends, coworkers (et al.).

Once you have found the gift you think he might like, wrap it according to your personal opinion on wrapping presents—but as a general rule with guys, "less (wrapping) is more," so don't overdo it. You are not looking for the expression on his face when he opens his (trinket) gift. You are looking to see what happens to it.

Does it end up on his desk, or did you spy some kid walking away with it a few minutes later? If the guy actually gives the present away to some random kid, you may want to ask him for the 10–20 bucks, and then tell him to lose your number. If you see it a few weeks later on his dashboard, bathroom counter, or in his workspace (basically anywhere he can get a few minutes of alone time, or anyplace he spends most of his day), you know that he likes to think of you often. This is generally "a good sign" if you like the guy.

If he returns the favor by buying you gifts (of approximately equal or greater value), you can bet that he will buy you bigger and bigger presents as you start to show a bit of appreciation, and return the favor occasionally in kind. What you don't want to see is him pulling away a few days after you give him a gift. Too many guys look at a gift from a girl as some form of entrapment, or a nesting urge. This little trick will show you whether the guy(s) you like suffer from this neurosis.

Instant Persuasion Tactics
*The amazing power of validating a guy's ego
casually, as if without even knowing that you did.*

Everyone likes getting a compliment, <u>especially if it reinforces some belief about ourselves that we want someone to notice,</u> or something we doubt we have, *but wish other people would think we do.* Compliments can fall in the realm of flattery or validation. I want to show you how to work your magic on ANY guy without anyone else catching on, by structuring your compliments to <u>validate his ego</u> (and make him dependent on you eventually, if you like) **rather than coming across as mindless, meaningless flattery.**

Flattery is simple. You tell someone something obvious about themselves. "Wow . . . you are pretty." How many times have you heard that? *B-o-r-i-n-g*. But I'll bet if a complete stranger approached you and complimented you on a hat you had just bought, remarking how unique it was, you would probably be deeply flattered (at least for a minute or two). This person has just told you that you look good—*and*—that you have excellent taste in hats.

If they happened to glance down at that moment at a letter you were writing and complimented you on your excellent penmanship, you would be racking up the compliments. Not a bad day after all. These two innocuous remarks could easily start a conversation and from there you may just end up making a new friend.

Try this experiment: Validate people by *casually* noticing something they did, or something they are, that is pleasing to you. Average guys get far too few compliments from women. This makes them suckers for a little attention and an offhand compliment *(which is often the <u>cause</u> of a LOT of trouble in relationships)*.

You can turn a man's head with a smile and a well placed compliment faster and more effectively than standing naked in front of him with a bottle of tequila. Appealing to a guy's libido is easy—just look at any porn star. But arousing a man is only going to make him want to have sex with you, not get him to do what you want.

If you want to win his heart and mind, you have to assault the heart and mind. Any reasonable compliment, subtly inserted into any conversation, will have the impact you want on just about any guy you meet. Forget the few exceptions for the moment; let's see what happens to a guy when you compliment him.

As an example, let's say there is an attractive guy at the office where you work. You see him getting coffee and casually tell him how great that suit looks on him. You have just told him that he is attractive, has good taste in suits, and that his desired effect of women thinking that he *is* attractive in that suit has just come to pass. Moreover, you have told him that *you* noticed.

This puts you above any other girl at the office who has not bothered to tell him directly that he looks good in his suits. All you have done is casually mention that you liked his suit—no big deal, right? But to him you have cemented your appreciation of him into his mind. Even if either of you is married, he will remember that you complimented him for quite some time, and he will look forward to seeing if you approve of his other decisions as well.

When you compliment someone on something they own, wear, or do and the compliment sticks in their mind, you in essence own them for a short period of time. This is *Marketing 101,* so watch out for people complimenting you when they want you to buy something. By the way, might I say that you showed *excellent taste* in purchasing a copy of this book. **Why not get an extra copy for a friend?**

If you place your compliment just right, you will create a subtle bond with the other person, one that you can build on. This is why guys like to tell you how pretty you look, and how well you do this or that. It's all a way to get you to be endeared to them *while they think of ways to get you to like them even more.* Everyone likes to feel good about themselves, but compliments can be manipulative.

So . . . the lesson for the day is that while it is more fun to get a compliment, *the real power is in giving sincere compliments.* Lavish praise on people you want to enslave—but do it skillfully, and watch the effect. When you find that a compliment fails to win someone over to you, it will usually be pretty obvious why.

Most important—When you give a compliment and it falls flat, simply add something "offhand" (as if you don't care that much) like: "Well, I thought so anyway," or "it's no big deal, I just think that you handled that well," and so on (this is depending on the situation). Then quickly, as if without a thought, change the subject to something you want to talk about.

If you *casually* compliment people on something (an event, an action, or something they own, or are wearing), they will almost always respond graciously. If you run into someone who views compliments with open contempt, *dismiss them immediately!*

Complimenting guys is easy, once you know what to look for. You can even use it as an icebreaker because of the average guy's susceptibility to being complimented by a woman. Most of the time he will start a conversation on the spot, allowing you to step back, relax, and watch him while he tries to impress you. Try it out—it's really easy! Compliment five guys tomorrow on something simple. Just say, *"Hey that's a nice ____."* You might even ask him where he got it. You will be amazed at how easily guys open up to you. Best of all, no one can accuse you of stealing men because you are just sharing a little kindness.

Remember the power of casual, yet sincere compliments, and use them often. Try complimenting someone you are in an argument with while they are ranting. If you are good, you will derail them instantly, and switch the conversation to the item. It's also a great way to end fights. You can always prove your point(s) later, when the other person is not so defensive.

Don't mistake "simplicity" for "easy"

It is said that "men want simplicity from women." Personaly, I disagree. Here is some simplicity:

You (to a guy who asks you out): "I only date men that earn over $100,000 a year."

THAT is simplicity. It is brutally simple. *Get a real job* and we will talk. I am not saying that you would say that. But if you did, it would be simple. What we really want is *easy*.

Here is easy:

You (to a guy who asks you out): "Tell you what: You go out and get some red wine and a couple of glasses. Please get glass, not plastic—it really makes a difference—oh, and while you are at it, grab a few candles and a blanket. I will whip up some snacks and meet you at the beach at sunset."

Not exactly simple, *but it is easy to understand,* and **easy for us to imagine** a date on the beach at sunset with you, and the date itself sounds easy. Low maintenance and fun—a guy's dream.

Guys, attention, affection, and sex . . .

I want to explode a myth. Being a guy, I have heard the popular belief that "all guys want/think about is sex," or that "guys think about sex 3,000 times a day." Nothing could be further from the truth. If all we thought about was sex, we would do anything women wanted—whenever you wanted us to do it, because all that would matter is that we got sex, sex, and more sex. We like sex, but even we are smart enough to realize that generally (for most guys at least) 3–5 times a week is *more* than enough.

In fact, once we are *actually having sex* on a *fairly regular basis* versus trying to impress our buddies by lying to them about how much sex we get, 1–2 times a day is **a lot**. That's 30–60 times a month! And, if you are doing it right, you don't have time for much of anything else (like sleeping, eating . . . forget work, or hanging out with the guys!).

You see we want more than sex—just like you do. We want time to work on our cars, time to hang out with our buddies—lying to them about how much sex we are getting—*time OFF of work*, and most important: we want **attention** *from women*. Sex is sex. It can be good, bad, or nonexistent, but the difference between getting sex, and getting *attention* is that one makes us feel good for a few hours and the other makes us feel like kings.

Any guy can get sex (even if he has to pay for it), but not every guy can walk around knowing that women (or even a woman he likes) actually like him, admire him, want to spend time with him, and shower him with affection—and every guy in the world knows this. That is our dirty little secret as men. That is what makes us secretly jealous of (and some of us actually angry at) you. <u>This feeling of disempowerment can only be corrected by a woman</u> (such as yourself) <u>fawning all over us</u>. This is why we spend our lives chasing after money, cars, power, whatever we think it will take for *you* to desire *us*, like *we* desire *you*.

Once a guy has convinced himself that women like him—that he can get attention from (almost) any woman he wants—his whole outlook changes. But for the rest of us, the "average guys" who still believe that the way to a girl's heart is through our wallet, the race to be popular (so you will like us), wealthy (so you will want us), and/or "sexy" (so you will lust after us) is on. We are suckers for attention: a smile (at us), a hello, a touch, and even you just *"being approachable."*

<u>Once you truly understand how endemic this is</u>, how it really does affect every man who strives to be a great athlete, a CEO, or a celebrity, and how it has affected you all of your life, you will see exactly how much power you have—if you choose to accept the power of your femininity. **This is not an apology for men.** Not at all! It is a cue to outwit them. Whenever you give a guy some of your attention (both the <u>quality</u> of your attention and the <u>amount of time spent</u> apply here), you validate his ego, you make him feel good to be a guy, and you have the chance to own a little piece of him. Because most guys invest so much of their time, energy, and money *chasing after girls,* they rarely get a chance to enjoy being the receiver of simple, casual affection and attention. Thus a little goes a long way (at least in the beginning).

105

We are (all) dependent on our luxuries. I know it sucks, but we are. Think about this for a moment:

Let's say you have a car (hopefully you do—this analogy works better that way). If you own a car, you can drive just about anywhere you want. No more walking! Screw that! Walking anywhere takes too long! Travel in style! So you have a car, and it is a nice car (a Lexus). It runs well, but you have to take it in to Jiffy Lube every 3,000 miles to make sure that it keeps running perfectly. Don't forget a weekly car wash (or detail job), premium gas, a safe place to park it, an alarm, monthly payments, *total coverage* insurance (the really expensive kind) . . . I think you get the idea. To pay for this car, *you have to work "x" number of hours a week* just to cover basic expenses. But it really is a nice car . . .

Be a luxury to the guy(s) you like. <u>Be something special</u>. Be "the girl who gives him attention and appreciates things about him no one else can see," *and watch him become dependent on you.*

Giving a guy you like at all just a little attention and affection **costs absolutely nothing** (so I know you can afford it), and 99% of the time will make him do nice things for you. The moment you think he is not making the monthly payments (not returning the affection, attention, appreciation, etc.), try breaking down (like your car) and see what happens. If the guy is really hooked, he will go insane. If he doesn't even seem to notice, then it's time to find a new guy. Life is too short to waste on idiots.

Using "action" to sway guys to your way of thinking

Guys thrive on action. This really is a "no-brainer" so I hope you already know this—and by "know this" I mean that <u>you actually work it into</u> your guy manipulating schedule. *Action,* as in action movies, action sports, action (like when are we going to ACTUALLY go on a date?!!) in all of its forms is important to guys. The exact opposite of action is stagnation (doing nothing until you get stale and rot like a tomato left in the sun for a few weeks; definitely not a pretty sight).

Guys need stimulus. We need to "do" things. It is part of being a guy. If you want to capture a guy's interest, be "active" when you are around him. "Talk is cheap." A guy invented that line. What he meant to say was "stop talking woman—let's *do* something!" *Action* is a quick way to seduce any man you like, or to get the attention of any man you want to to know more about.

If we see you as a girl "who likes to do things," you will be invited places, to do things. Women who are too high maintenance, or take too long to get ready to go anywhere—and especially the ones who complain about everything once they get there—are quickly labeled, and stop getting invited anywhere.

Adventure: How to get more fun out of life—and your men (or man)

Action is something you do every day. Adventure is a way of life. A life without adventure is really boring. Our technological advances have turned us all soft and squishy. Here is something that should give you a laugh. Think about this the next time some guy flexes his muscles in front of you:

<u>We have someone else butcher our meat for us</u>, and then cut it up into neat little packages with that white foam (or yellow for chicken) with clear plastic wrap over the top. Packaging is great. It makes food look so easy to cook. I like packaging with a picture of what the food "should look like after you cook it" (if you are a professional chef, and have fancy plates on hand).

Back when grandma (or great-grandma) had to chase Mr. Chicken around the yard shouting at it to stand still, <u>making dinner was something of an adventure</u>. Going to fetch water meant the possibility of being eaten by a crocodile, or finding buried treasure *(well, it COULD happen)*. Now everything we need in life is ready-made for us. A quick trip to the store to buy soap, toilet paper, and whatever else we might need for the week is capped off by the age-old dilemma of "paper or plastic?"

The most adventure we get is fighting traffic. No wild lands to tame, forests to slash and burn, native tribes to wipe off the planet, no more cute little fluffy forest animals to hunt into extinction. We don't even have mice running around the kitchen anymore. So we look for adventure anywhere we can get it.

Guys like action movies because we like watching some other guy get the crap beat out of him for a few hours. It is a catharsis to the complete lack of adventure in our own lives. Then there is the (minimalistic) plotline we try to lose ourselves in so we can pretend that we are in that world.

The same basic premise works for sports on TV, except that we are more like cheerleaders*. Not much of a substitute for adventure, but it works for most guys.

Tell your favorite guy that he looks like a cheerleader shouting at the TV while the REAL MEN are busy playing the sport he is watching. It won't make him like you, but it is hilarious to watch him try to deny it.

Anything in life can be an adventure if you look at it from the right perspective. Getting lost can be an adventure. If you can look at solving any problem you are confronted with as an adventure, then you are well on your way to an exciting life. Start by going over your various lists and reminding yourself what your passions are.

What is important enough (to you) to get up from the TV long enough to do, learn, or create something? Your passions will take you on many adventures. Your first adventure may even be discovering how you can pursue your passion. You may have to track down resources and materials to follow your dreams.

Creative projects can liven up even the most boring lives, turning routine into an experience that will create memories that last a lifetime. Take a video camera with you on a weekend excursion. Film your funniest moments and edit them with some free software you can get on the Internet. Buy a book at a local bookstore and learn how to make paper, learn how to play the tambourine and join a punk band. Find something in your area and drag the men in your life to it. If you can't think of anything to do, pick up any of your town's newspapers and look in the activities section for ideas. Your life is waiting for you to start doing something with it.

Go to the library or bookstore and scour the arts and crafts section, *just for inspiration.* This is your life. It is up to you to make it fun. Guys will promise you the sun and the moon, but if you really want those things, you will have to become the type of woman that attracts the kind of men who can deliver.

The moral of the story is that real men like real adventure, and the rest like whatever passes for adventure at the time. It makes us feel like we are living the dream in a vicarious way. So . . . if you can provide your men with a life of adventure—*or at least enhance their adventure*—rather than whine and complain about how they are not spending enough time with you, you will find that men love you, and other women hate you.

Guys who know you will be nagging their girlfriends and wives that they should be more like *you.* You will become the dream girl to men everywhere. From there you can choose the one(s) you want to share good times, and many adventures, with.

How to keep a man faithful

First, do not give him any reason to doubt you. Get inside his head and see how emotionally stable he is, preferably before you get too serious with him. Find out what baggage he carries around with him wherever he goes. Are women just "Bitches" 'n "Ho's" to him? Is every woman (but his mom) a tramp? Does he even like his mother? Does he have any sisters? Does he talk to them? How many of his ex-girlfriends (or ex-wives) cheated on him? These are questions you want answers to before you let him start claiming any kind of exclusivity on you.

If you decide his baggage weighs less than yours (always a good sign), you have a good start. If you seriously believe that the man you have your eyes set on desires you enough to be monogamous, look to his character. Test it. You cannot trust a man with your heart if he has no character. If he is constantly looking for shortcuts in life, or looking to blame other people for his personal dilemmas, you can be sure to be next. A lot of the process of keeping a man faithful is *not choosing the wrong men to begin with.*

That being said, you need to know:

Why guys cheat

(This is not an excuse—it is just a list of the most common reasons)

1: <u>They are bored</u> (with you, and too afraid to leave)

—The sex is bland.

—The sex is rare.

—The sex is not as good as it used to be.

—They don't like you as much as they used to.

—They are consciously or subconsciously comparing you (unfairly) to some girl at work . . .

1a: <u>They are bored</u> (with themselves, but through the magic of emotional transference, **you get the blame**—and isn't that nice?)

—They hate their life.

—They are jealous of their friend(s) that they feel have something "better" than they do (a better job, car, girlfriend?).

—They feel stifled, so by having sex with another woman they are "getting back at life" or "recharging their batteries" (unfortunately at your expense).

2: <u>They feel invalidated</u> (by you)

—They feel that you get so much *more attention* than they do, <u>that they have to prove how sexy they are</u> (to themselves) by cheating on you.

—They believe that you don't give them enough attention or affection. *This includes touching them on a regular basis,* back rubs, bringing them a snack, beer, cooking meals . . .

—You two argue too much.

(Continued on next page . . .)

3: <u>They are incapable of being loyal</u>

About one in fifty men suffer from this condition. <u>Choose someone better next time</u>. This kind of guy is easy to spot if you are paying attention to messages he is broadcasting *rather than the pretty words and empty promises he uses to wear down your resistance to him.* Your friends are useful in helping you spot guys like this before you get too involved with them.

An old story* tells of a scorpion who sat at the bank of a river wanting to get across to the other side. The story has a few variations, depending on who tells it, but here is the gist of it:

The scorpion spies a fox who is about to cross the river and calls out, "Hey Mister Fox, I need to cross this river and I cannot swim! Perhaps I can ride on your back as you cross and we can both arrive safely on the other side, where we can part ways and proceed to our destinations."

The fox is no fool however. He replies that he knows of the scorpion, and his nature of stabbing things indiscriminately with his tail, which is alleged to carry a deadly poison that kills within seconds. He accuses the scorpion of plotting to inject him with poison along the way, to which our erudite friend retorts, "Why that would be madness! Surely we would both drown! Come off this logic and let us cross, so that we may both keep our appointments."

The fox acquiesces, and the scorpion hops on the fox's back, grabbing hold of some of the fox's fur with his tiny pincers to keep from falling into the water. As expected, about halfway across the stream, the scorpion just can't resist temptation and repeatedly jabs the fox viciously in the back with the stinger on his tail, each time dosing him with massive amounts of his deadly venom. The fox cries out in alarm, asking why the scorpion would do such a thing.

True to form, the scorpion replies, *"I cannot help it. It is who I am."* And they both drown.

* This tale appears as *The Scorpion and the Fox* (or *Toad, Frog,* and so on). The scorpion usually "wins" <u>except in the version entitled</u> *The Scorpion and the Tortoise,* wherein the tortoise's shell is too hard for the scorpion to penetrate. In *that* version of the tale, the

tortoise informs the scorpion that he has earned his own demise through his treachery and returns the favor by sinking under the water, *thereby drowning the ungrateful little bastard.*

This fable is credited to several authors, most notably Bidpai, although even that factoid is suspect. In my retelling of the version, I have made the victim a fox, because they are cute, and the scorpion eloquent, because it makes him look all the more evil to have such command of an intricate thought.

Your man will act according to his nature.

No matter how intelligent (or not), **he will be driven by his desires and instincts.** "Actions speak louder than words." Never forget that when a guy tells you a-n-y-t-h-i-n-g.

How to plant a suggestion in a guy's mind

Oh sure, casually mention how a (male) coworker introduced you to a new lunch hotspot and thirty seconds later your boyfriend is all but accusing you of having an affair with everyone at work. But tell him that you want to take a month off work to travel Europe with him and he starts whining about his work schedule, lack of time, and the cost of long-term parking at the airport. Have you ever had trouble getting your point across to a guy? Do you feel that guys don't listen to what you say?

Don't worry: it's not him—*it's you.*

Stop fighting nature. A man's mind works the way it does, and if you knew how to navigate the twists and turns of the male ego as it wends its way through logic circuits, you could have any-thing that you desired in life handed to you on a silver platter *(or a platinum platter, if your tastes are as extravagant as mine tend to run on occasion)* by a gentleman in a tuxedo with a white towel draped across his left forearm. Nevertheless, it is clear that you are in need of:

world's only "The instant course to implanting suggestions in men's heads!"

The *easiest* way to get a guy to do anything is to make him think that if he does this one thing, women in general (or that a particular girl he likes) *will think he is a complete stud, throw themselves at him*—even fight over him. **Yes—we are that stupid.** Why do you think we start wars, or do any number of other stupid things with our money, time, and fists?

The most important thing to a guy (after things like breathing, eating, and occasionally being forced to sleep) is having women adore him. Sure—too many of you think that we are busy chasing you. Perish the thought. **We are not THAT stupid.** We know all too well that in order for us to be happy, *we need your attention, and affection.* We need you to look at us and think we are superstars, even gods among men. You know this. It's time that you started using this knowledge to get what you want, without having to nag, beg, or wait for us to get around to it.

As you are not going to chase us down, fight over us, and throw yourselves at our feet (or at least not without a little begging on our part), we figure we might as well let you know how great we are—*so that you will do all of these things.* Failing that, most of us simply agree to give up a little of our pride, time, energy, and money; becoming "a provider." By showering you with attention, gifts, food, money, and alcohol, we hope to make you think of us as amazing.

We gladly put up with crappy jobs, asshole bosses, and long hours at work for a few quality hours with you; because when it comes down to it, a few hours with a girl we like is worth all of "that other stuff." This is how it has been throughout history. We know deep down in our hearts that you probably like some other guy better than us, but that doesn't matter, as long as you don't tell us.

All that matters is that we get you to like us enough to spend time with us and give US the attention and affection we crave. Too many of us (men) settle for just having you around—and having sex—

113

<u>when what we really want is for you to adore us</u>. This is the foundation of most of the world's problems. Men need to "man up" and start telling women what they want to be happy. Until they do, however, someone has to take the reins of any relationship and guide it to happier places.

If you are going to get men *to want to do* what you want them to do, <u>*you must apply*</u> the basic techniques of marketing. Corporations spend billions of dollars every year researching how to get men to buy their products and services. Their findings only reinforce what Delilah knew a few thousand years ago. Appeal to the man's ego and libido. Appeal to his heart (mend it or break it).

<u>Men</u> <u>will</u> <u>willingly</u> hand over their wallet to you, the keys to their house, car, safe-deposit box, etc., *if you simply make them feel better for doing so,* than any other woman. This happens every day to men all over the planet. Men don't even think this through most of the time. It is amost always an instinctual "need" to surrender their conquests and treasures to the woman they crave. Some men will lord their wealth and power over women because they have no respect for them, but they are easy enough to spot and avoid. On a regular basis, the men you meet will give a part of their lives and their resources to any women who inspire them. It really would be a shame if you missed out on all of the fun.

Do NOT rely solely on sex or sexuality or you will lose eventually. **There will always be** someone younger, "hotter," more fun, smarter, or funnier <u>than all of us</u>. That is the way life works. We all have our turn on stage. The trick is to not be threatened by anyone else. **You have unique strengths that you can draw on** to get men to see things your way.

Men will fight you for every inch of ground when it comes to who gets to decide what "we" (you and "us") will do. But you will always have the final trump card—*your affection, appreciation, and acceptance.* If you have laid the groundwork for all of your interactions with men by developing all of the aspects of your femininity, you will find men easy to sway to your point of view.

In a guy's mind . . .
The perfect wife

Age 15

Dude . . . *what are you talking about?*

. . . oh, you mean like *my mom* or something?

Dude . . . yeah, whatever. Maybe when I'm too old to get a date.

Age 21

Actually meeting the fantasy girl from "Age 21 perfect girlfriend" *(page 78)*

Age 30

Sexy, and still likes sex *with you*

Responsible, financially prudent (hasn't maxed out the credit cards)

A good mother, but not obsessed with having too many kids

Still makes you feel important, and sexy

Appreciates sacrifices you make for her

Age 50+

Stopped nagging you ten years ago

Puts out occasionally

Pretends she likes it

Still makes breakfast

Can actually cook

Keeps to herself when you are working on your hobbies

Makes you feel wanted

Section 4

Guys:

Other Important Stuff

How to tell the jerks
from the decent guys
upon first meeting them

Inasmuch as every guy can be a jerk on certain days, there are just some guys who feel a need to be assholes to everyone, every day, because deep down they are afraid that someone will come along and assault their masculinity. Even worse, there are a small handful of men who are truly evil, men who enjoy making other people miserable, but these men are few and far between. So unless you date politicians, you generally don't have to worry about them.

Whether you want to attract or avoid the jerks and assholes of your locale, these tips should make spotting them a lot easier. First, heed the advice of your friends. Of course, your friends are not always right and, in fact, they are wrong just as often as you are; but all of us have better vision when we are looking at someone else's problems, instead of our own. So when you are checking out guys, it's a good idea to get a "second opinion" before you get too serious.

But let's say that your friends are all busy fending off jerks of their own, and there's no way you can get any help figuring out who is good for you, and who is just "making nice" to get something out of you. How can you spot a prince in a room full of clowns?

Believe it or not, most jerks will purposely send clear messages that they are bad for you. They are so used to bullying everyone that it only makes sense for them to broadcast their intention to find a girl who will "shut up and do what they are told." They use this tactic *because it works*. There seems to be a never-ending supply of women who mistake this attitude for "strength" or virility.

There are also a growing number of books on "how to pick up girls" that *perpetually reinforce* **the need to** *demean women* in order to have sex with them. By teaching their students to belittle you and actively destroy ANY self-love and confidence you may have, these authors seek to *make you believe* that you are lucky to have sex with a loser who is openly insulting you. If you are looking for someone to tell you what to do, this makes these men easy to spot. Ignore the rest of the guys; they will only bore you.

A step below the openly "Hey look at me everyone! I am an Alpha Bully!" males, you will spot their friends, the "I could not possibly care less about you or your needs" charmers. Also a very popular selection on our menu—*highly recommended*. These guys will generally be friendly, smile, and charm you, but you will know instantly where they stand when they make decisions for you; and when you show resistance, they will shrug you off like a coat on a hot day. The inference will be that they are going to have a good time, with or without you, and unless you want to spend your time wondering what you missed out on, you had better jump on the ride while it lasts.

This pattern of "Hey, enjoy the ride or get off, but don't complain" will continue throughout your relationship. These guys aren't bad *per se*. But they will set the rules for you to follow, and the more you argue on a regular basis, the more unhappy they will make you, until they dump you for a more pliable woman. *With rare exception, you cannot tame these guys.*

It is best to take a supportive, adventurous mindset in dealing with them to get what you want. Be there to enjoy the fun when you want, on your terms, *and challenge them by inviting them along on adventures of your own design.* This will get you the best positioning possible—where you will be revered above all other women they know, but not relegated to subservience.

The majority of men that you see on a daily basis *(whether they approach you or not)* will fall into the next category: These guys are pretty clueless about women. Sure they are great accountants, mechanics, salesmen, or artists*, but that is because they spent years of their lives studying, practicing, and perfecting their skills, because their existence depended on their abilities to perform.

Women are generally secondary to career in the psyche of the working-class male. Women don't pay the rent after all. **The boss does.** *(Yeah, yeah, I know all about your good-for-nothing-no-job-having-musician ex-boyfriend. I'm not talking about him at the moment.)*

* *"artists"—generically meaning artists, musicians, actors, writers of all types, and so on . . .*

These guys have varying degrees of skill in dealing with women, but all the years they spent honing their skills in their chosen pro-fession *were years they did not, on average, spend learning how to deal with women.* So they do what they can. When these guys are jerks, it is because they are lashing out defensively.

Someone either convinced them that "women like bad boys," and so they are trying that hat on for size—*or*—one of their ex's burned them pretty bad, and they are still carrying around some baggage. On the nicer side of the spectrum, you will find the guys who hold doors open for you, and generally look for ways to help make your day a little brighter, or easier, without making a big deal of trying to get anything from you in return.

We call these guys suckers. You might call them "nice guys," but we doubt that you call them at all—except when you need a ride home at 2 a.m. from a party because your date took off with some other girl.

Quick Example:

The player will open the door for you and say (as you pass), "You are looking fine today," and once you smile, he follows up with a line that is designed to get your phone number—or an instant date. No big deal. Fairly straightforward stuff.

The "nice guy" will do everything about the same, but instead of going for the kill (date or number), <u>he will stand there like an idiot</u> and smile, waiting for you to give him your number "if you are interested," *or worse,* he will walk away, thinking how he made someone's day a little nicer.

Bah! It's a wonder nice guys finish at all. The guys who ask you out most often are the ones who are consumed with figuring out how to get you to stop living your life—and start living your life *around them.*

Of course every once in a while, a truly decent guy will get so horny, or <u>enamored with you</u> (it's usually the former, but there's always hope) that he makes a complete idiot of himself pursuing you, just like the "hero" in those cheesy romantic comedies you drag us to see.

At the far end of the spectrum we have the desperate, the insane (stalkers), and the guys who will say anything you want to hear to win your heart (or panties). The fringes always serve as haven for the lunatics, whether the fringe is religion, politics, or dating.

When a guy is just "too nice," *run.* In fact, run away fast. There is a minute possibility that he is the nicest guy you would ever want to meet, but even if he is, you would get bored with him in a few weeks anyway. More than likely he is deeply disturbed, or hasn't had a date in so long that he will do anything to get one. NOT a good sign. Proceed at your own risk.

It is an amazingly good idea to find out how much and what type of baggage your chosen guys have, and how long they plan on carrying it around, before you get all loopy over them. <u>The time to ask these questions is early on,</u> while we are *blindly obsessed* with pleasing you so that you, in turn, will give us all kinds of affection. We are most malleable at the beginning of the relationship. Always use that to your advantage.

Just in case you ever wondered . . .

How to get a woman elected President of The United States

Okay . . . so this is like, going to sound really simple, but it works—I promise: Vote. Yeah, I know, that means missing whatever is on TV on Tuesday night, but just TiVO your favorite shows and get your friends out to vote as well. Make a party of it. Lie to them and tell them that there will be "hot guys" there. It's your country. *If you want to see some common sense in this world,* you have to stop what you are doing on election day, and get out there and vote. It really does make a difference. It will make a difference that you can see in your life. Best of all, it's free! Women around the world still do not have the right to vote, **but the statistics tell us that** *most* **young women in this country** don't even bother.

If you are tired of men making decisions for you, stop the cycle and vote—just once every 2 years. Men have been making decisions for you ever since you were born. Men vote. Almost all senators and congressmen are men; **EVERY President has been a man.** *The bottom line is that men tell you what to do every day, and you don't even realize it.*

I will say this again: **If you are tired of men telling you what to do, deciding how much you will get paid, and what YOU can do with YOUR body:** *vote.*

Just one day every 2 years. I don't even care how you vote—only that you do. Do it just three times (that means 3 days over a 6 year period) *and make sure you drag two or three friends with you,* kicking and screaming if you have to. Take them out for drinks afterwards (make the guys pay of course). I promise you will see a difference. Don't be embarrassed if most of the initiatives are confusing. Men write them that way *so that you won't vote.*

Everyone is confused on election day. That is why we all get pretty coupons in the mail telling us how to think (and vote). If nothing else, at least make sure you vote for all of the women candidates. Of course, don't be so silly as to *tell anyone* that I told you to do all of this. I like my head attached to my body.

How to SERIOUSLY
attract rich guys

Okay . . . I am feeling a bit guilty for making you read that rant about why it is vitally important for you to participate in our democracy so that guys stop making decisions for you behind your back. So, I will expand on this a bit. There are a *lot of ways to do this*. Keep to everything I have taught you, and be sure to practice your smiles. Be sure to read the parts about making elitism sexy, and also read "Are you worth two month's salary?"

In fact, read the whole book. Read it three times, and practice everything carefully and thoroughly on the men in your life. Use all of these techniques on your guy "friends" _until you are confident that you can get men to do exactly what you want on a regular basis_. While you are at it, get another copy of this book for your friends who keep asking you "how you do it."

Then take your sexy-self to areas where rich guys congregate. Stay away from the expensive nightclubs. You will just get played there. Visit yacht and country clubs, high-rises, and luxury car dealerships. Pretend that you are lost, or inquiring for your boss, brother, father.

Use all of your skills on the men there, and you will soon find yourself welcomed into the inner circles of powerful men (or at least to their parties). From there on, I think you will figure out what to do. Test your skills on married men if you like, because they are the easiest marks. Flirt casually if you like, but be careful. Once a social-climbing woman bags her very own rich guy, she can be insanely jealous. Married rich guys often cheat, because they became wealthy in the first place *to get female attention*.

I do not advocate cheating with a married guy (wealthy or not). But that's just me. You will do what you think is best at the moment. Just remember that while married rich guys are fun to flirt with, and great practice for sharpening your skills, they can play you like a fiddle. If you want a rich guy of your own, it is best to find someone who is "up and coming" versus the perpetual player, unless you don't mind sharing him.

How to win your argument
but not lose your guy

Arguments suck. But every once in a while it seems we all need to yell at someone to stay sane. Don't ask me why—I'm a guy. We just do things; we don't sit around and wonder why. Anyway, it seems to be most satisfying when we (all of us, not just the guys) get to yell at someone we deeply care about, because we all yell at people we love more than we do complete strangers.

Who designed our existing relationship structure anyway? If you know them, whap them upside the head with a large brick for doing such a bad job. In the meantime, here is how to win arguments *and make yourself look good to anyone who might be watching* in the process.

Validate, validate, validate. I know, it sucks. In an argument, all you want to do is rip the other person's head off for being such an argumentative idiot. If you don't, you are not putting enough passion into your words. But actually "winning" an argument means not only getting your point across, but coming out looking like a good person. If you can get the person you are arguing with <u>to think you are a good person *after the argument*,</u> then you have mastered the art of positive manipulation, even when you are angry. This is a skill that will make dealing with guys (any guy) a lot easier—or at least more enjoyable.

So about this "validation" thing. Validating anything (in an argument anyway) is simply pausing for a moment to point out that you agree with what was just said, or complimenting someone on their delivery, even if their message was malicious. When you do this, you stop the other person just long enough to point out your impression of what they just said ("Well, *that* definitely makes sense.") and, if necessary, encourage them to continue if they stare at you bewildered. You are softening their stance by injecting a sincere compliment or agreement, and simultaneously showing yourself to be a compassionate and intelligent person. Your ability to calmly pick out one or two things, at various points (as they arise), that you can agree with does more than build a bridge between the two of you (so you can end this argument quickly). You are also stealing some of the fight out of them.

You are not escalating the argument; *you are dematerializing it*. The fact that you can see ANY of their side (no matter how ridiculous it may seem at the moment), *subtly puts you in control* of the argument by relegating it to a "point-by-point discussion" of the issues at hand. You become the defacto moderator, even though you are also a participant in the argument.

If the other person follows your lead, all the better. Don't be threatened if they try to one-up you by turning your complimenting strategy around on you (they start complimenting you), or they suddenly decide to drop the argument altogether. If they do this, quietly pat yourself on the back, and make the best of it.

<u>It may not be as much fun</u> discussing things calmly as it is throwing knives and shouting obscenities, but it makes people like you more, especially people who have money to spend on you. Here is a quick example of using validation in an argument:

You: *Blah, blah, blah (all valid points I am sure, but as guys—we aren't listening very closely anyway).*

Me: Here's the problem:* Your "guy friends" just want to have sex with you. The reason they do nice things for you is because they are just waiting for their turn in line.

You: *What?!! You jealous, self-centered, insecure, controlling <u>asshole</u>!! Do you think I am some kind of <u>turnstile</u> that men can have a go at if they form a line?*

(Oops! Wow that was fun to say—and maybe even true, but let's try a <u>slightly different</u> tactic.)

You: *What? (breathe . . .) Look . . . I'm sure there are a lot of guys who would want to have sex with me—or with ANY girl for that matter—but that doesn't mean they have a chance in hell. The reason I <u>haven't</u> had sex with them is because I have <u>no interest in them</u>.*

See how you used <u>my point</u> to make <u>yours more valid</u>? Note that you didn't use my words *against me*. You used them as "a possibility" and said (in effect) that <u>even if I am correct</u>, you have no interest in the guys I am accusing you of potentially having sex with. But we're not through yet!

Me: Yeah, but I know for a fact that Ryan is trying to steal you away. He stole Greg's girlfriend at the party last Saturday—

You: *Yeah, I know about that. You're right, he's a real slimeball . . .*******

Please take a moment and think about this. Once you do this, you have changed the dynamics from an argument to *a discussion of the issue at hand*. What you have done (to us) is removed all of the "You are (blah blah, blah) bitch!" and replaced it with "This is what is bothering me, and you . . . you . . . agree . . . *bitch!*" (Sorry, I just couldn't help myself.)

---

* "Here's the problem:" <u>This is an unfair arguing tactic</u>. I have stated that what I am about to say is the central issue, and that you have to pay attention to what I am about to say. Instead of just saying it, I have packed my argument into a cannon with extra gunpowder, so I can launch my point at you with *extra force*. The end result is that what I say sounds more antagonistic and, therefore, just escalates the fight. Watch out for tactics like this in an argument.

** You confirmed information I told you (*"Yeah, I know about that"*), **and validated my opinion** (*"you are right"* and *"he's a real slimeball"*) **twice.** Only a complete idiot guy would continue arguing with you at this point. You have put us on the same team. We are simply bringing different points of view to the table.

At this point, if the guy you are arguing with sees this *as weakness on your part,* and decides to press his attack, <u>you need to show him</u> how you agreed with him on a few specific points. Then tell him that if he doesn't *back off a bit,* **and stop pressuring you,** that you are going to see this as a <u>character flaw</u>—something that will lower your desire to even be around him, much less have any (sexual) interest in him.

Sometimes you need to get in your guy's face and let him know that bad behavior will not be tolerated, or he will stomp all over you. It's a sad fact, but you will more than likely have to teach the men in your life to argue fairly; but once trained, the good ones will be much easier to deal with.

By agreeing with *anything* we have said, and/or complimenting us on our delivery of a point, you have started to wear away our resistance *to hearing your points,* and proven to us how considerate you are, even in an argument. It really gives you an unfair advantage, but half of us will be too stupid to notice and the other half will not be able to complain, because what you did was a positive thing. Use this to your advantage whenever you can.

This technique is intimately related to its evil twin: *"Oh no you didn't! You did NOT just say . . ."* The interruption of our point to insert a comment of your own <u>is the same gut reaction</u>. The difference is that instead of something indignant coming from you, we get a compliment. *That is the last thing anyone is expecting* when they are trying to bully someone into hearing what they have to say. The effect can completely stop someone in their tracks, and even stun them into silence.

This level of "intelligence meets kindness" is all but impossible to find among people these days. By making yourself an exceptional human being, <u>you start to attract more evolved men</u>. With practice, you will find arguments with (just about) anyone easier to solve, while feeling that you can get your points across when you need to most (during a shouting match).

This is an infinitely better method of handling disagreements than simply "giving in" because you are tired of being berated. You gain respect, teach the other person to be civil when disagreeing with you, and you walk away feeling like you got to say your peace rather than feeling run over by a bully. **Practice looking for individual points you can agree with in other people's arguments,** especially the guys you date. Casually mention that you agree, without derailing them. Say something like *"Yeah, I agree with that . . ."* instead of *"That one thing, right there, I agree with."*

Also, if the other person takes your agreement as a license to steamroll you, bullying you into agreeing with other points (e.g., they think you are caving in), take a deep breath, call a time out, or just walk away *and refuse to let them pressure you.* If all else fails, point out how you "are willing to work through this discussion," but that you have no interest in being pushed around verbally. Unless the other person is a complete asshole, they should stop for a moment and agree that you are right, and calm down a bit.

Logic

Guys love to use "logic" in arguments. It gives us a platform, or a fulcrum if you like. You see, way back in history, some big strong Greek guy named Atlas once boasted, "Give me a lever long enough, and I can lift *the world.*" Fortunately, someone was standing nearby with a pen and a scroll to jot that down, in case they ever wanted to take him up on that challenge in a tavern.

By using logic <u>as a wedge</u> to strengthen our presentation, we believe we can gain some level of authority in an argument. As men, we are brainwashed to obey authority figures. **Authority means power.** Power means freedom, control, *basically the ability to do whatever we want.* This is why men like to be the boss in relationships. Freedom, power, autonomy—who needs teamwork?

So naturally, we do whatever we can to get some of that authority and power for ourselves. Using logic to make our argument *sound obvious,* and therefore inarguable, is our way of getting what we want easily (remembr, we *like* "easy"). Here is the problem with that:

<u>Logic works best when it is based on absolutes</u>. Computers function on absolutes. Everything inside a computer breaks down to a 1 or a 0, yes or no, "on" or "off." Therefore, to a computer, something either *is* or it is *not. There is never a "well . . . maybe . . ."* This is the perfect foundation for logic.

<u>In a guy's mind</u>, "logic" is guided by personal bias. Our opinions shape our "logic." What we like to call logic is really nothing more than a collection of facts carefully chosen to support our beliefs. This doesn't make us *wrong,* in most cases—but at best, our truth is colored by our opinions. We like using logic to support our claims because it removes anyone's ability to argue with us. If it is "logical," <u>then we must do it</u> *(e.g., have casual sex with all of your attractive friends).*

What this means: When we try to use logic to pressure you into doing something we want, you will understand the facts we are presenting, but the story as a whole will often sound fishy. We will use "logic" to prevent you from arguing with us, expecting you to cave in if we just apply enough pressure.

Too many men think that all we need is a bigger lever to get you to do what we want, when we want it. This is an indication that we think you are weak-minded, and can be controlled. If you see this as a pattern in the men you date, stop dating idiots.

If you try to explain all of this to a guy you are dating, you are asking for a fight. Even if we agree with you, we will still search for some platform to prove that we are right, some crutch to support us.

130

Most guys have not figured women out—*at all*—and, therefore, believe that you have some sort of unfair advantage. These guys point to all of the men who will do *anything* to get attention from women as proof that they are right.

It is best to know these things and *understand why* guys do the things that we do, *even if we don't*. This makes us **much** easier to deal with. But dissecting us (to our face), destroys our value to you—and that is where our egos get bruised . . . and the trouble starts.

Okay, that was a lot to absorb, so here is a quick summary: When you are in an argument, look for points where you can agree, and point them out quickly and casually (don't make a big deal of it, but make sure that we know). This makes YOU look like a better person to us (and anyone else around), and stops us from monopolizing the conversation.

Also, when you can see ways to lower the tension level, *do it*. There is no sense letting some guy ruin your day by getting you so angry that you can't blow it off quickly and easily. **This also puts you in control,** and that feels good in an argument. When a guy plays the logic card, validate facts when you can, but don't let him bully you.

If nothing else, tell him to hold on a second, take a breath to collect yourself, and tell him that you want *some time to think about this* (this is his cue to shut up and stop pressuring you). Whether you give the argument another moment's thought doesn't matter. You politely got him to shut up, and now you can think about what you want to say, or you can put the whole argument off for some other day.

You can tell a lot about a guy by the way he argues, and the words he uses. Early on in a relationship, most guys will avoid arguments if they don't want to scare you away. If a guy *abuses* logic when he is trying to get you to see his point or do something he wants, take this as a red flag and don't walk—*run* away fast.

The same holds true for any guy who attacks you verbally in an argument, pointing out how inferior you are. These are signs that the guy is deficient. He needs to be sent back. You might still be able to get a refund.

131

How to string a guy along
(for later use)

Bah! I'm going to get so much crap for this, but I did have to call the book, *"How to Get ANY MAN to do ANYTHING You Want,"* so here goes:

Look . . . sometimes you will find a guy you like, or think you might like, but for whatever reason you aren't quite ready for him just yet. But letting him get stolen away by some other chippie is simply out of the question, so you need to string him along a bit. What follows should NOT be used on a guy you are dating; only guys you don't want to miss out on, once you have finished doing whatever it is that you need to do to know if you want him as yours for a while. Imagine you are getting ready for a date with a guy you like, and he arrives early. Great! Well, at least you know that *he will show up,* and you know where he is. You still need another 30 minutes to get ready (for whatever reason). So you need him to stay out of trouble, but not leave. This is "just like that."

It's best to have a good grasp of the basics here. Remember that a guy—*any guy*—will wait forever for the perfect woman. Fortunately, you don't want him to wait "forever," just a little while, so you don't have to be perfect; just be what he wants more than he wants someone else at the moment. You will be working on his heart, his pride, and his need to be a protector (of you), provider (for you), and/or his need for your unique companionship. If a guy thinks that *you alone understand him,* then you have already won him, and just need to keep him from getting away. If he is not there yet, this is where we are going to get him. The ideal emotional state we are looking to put him in is that there is something unique and special about you that hooks him like a fish.

Just for a moment, think of your favorite song. Your favorite song has several hooks in it. "Hooks" are those parts of a song that get stuck in your head all day—even if you hate the rest of the song. Usually the more hooks a song has, the more popular it will be. A hook in a song can be any twist of words, a clever phrase, a catchy melody, even a complete STOP! and then resumption of the beat. James Brown was the undisputed Grand Master of song hooks.

The term "hook" comes from fishing, where you put some bait (like a worm) on a bent piece of metal, and once "Mr. Fish" tries to eat the free worm, he becomes "Mr. Lunch." He gets hooked. Fishermen have funny hats. Their hats have their favorite hooks around the sides, so they can grab one (if the fish steals one) without having to wade back to shore and look in their tackle box. With all of those hooks hanging off the sides of the hat, you wouldn't want to sit on it. In fact, if you get too close to it, you will probably get caught up in one or two hooks.

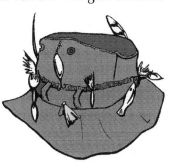

So, now imagine yourself as your favorite song. You have sprouted hooks all over you, like a porcupine with fishhooks for quills.

But just to make sure that you have enough hooks, we are going to give you a fishing hat too. That's better. Now, if any hot guy comes within twenty feet, he will be all tangled up in you.

So where do we get all of these hooks? We look to exploit the parts of your personality that attract men, parts you already possess. What is it about you that is going to turn men's heads, cloud their minds, and make them follow you home? Your "hooks" are made up of anything a guy might find beautiful, sexy, emotionally attractive, or in any way desirable about you. These are things you have to figure out for yourself, and then work on them. Build them up. Find your most powerful hooks, and then your minor ones. Sometimes men will ignore your largest, and most deadly hooks, only to get snagged by one you didn't even know you had. Let me give you some examples, but after that *what you really need is some homework.* I want you to start watching women wherever you go (like you don't already). Ask yourself "what's so attractive about *her?*" whenever you see a girl getting attention from a guy. Not all hooks are visible (as you will see), but after you get a little practice picking apart what other women rely on, you will be able to see all kinds of "hooks" women put out to snag passing men.

Once you can do this, it is time to start checking out the guys. Look at them and ask yourself, "What are they pushing?" What aspect of themselves are they trying to say to me: "Hey I am sexy <u>because of this</u>"? Don't skip over this part—or read it and think "yeah, that's nice," or "I'll get back to this." **Fold this page.** Highlight these paragraphs if you have to. Whatever you do, <u>make sure that you come back and read your homework assignment over and over</u> *until you see the words in your sleep.*

IF YOU DO THIS: First, you will learn to hate me. Not to worry. I have a few ex-girlfriends who already do, so you are in very good company. *Second,* you will become extremely adept at reading people, seeing what they think is "hot" about themselves, and what they wished you wouldn't look at. Once you know this, you will be able to manipulate anyone. Of course, I will ask you not to be harsh in your judgment of people, as we all have to get through the day the best we can. But it will be interesting to see how different people attract others. When you are so good that you can see through men's "game," you might even consider teaching your skills to other women (and making a tidy little income from that).

So, as promised, examples:

What are your natural talents, especially talents that you have honed with p-r-a-c-t-i-c-e? Can you sing, act, dance, draw, paint, *play ANY instrument?* You know how much we idolize celebrities. Even something as simple as singing in the church choir (if you are good) can get you noticed. And if you can sing in the choir, you can certainly get your self drunk enough to take a stab at karaoke, American Idol . . .

If you can act, draw, sew, or swing a hammer, you can join a theater troupe. Every city everywhere has a group of people who put on plays. Start anywhere. If you can sew AND act, do both, or even just sew costumes and set pieces while you search for the right part for you. Your contributions and team spirit will make you popular. Popular girls get more guys to choose from.

If you can COOK, then make sure you get practice, *a lot of practice.* Volunteer for your church or any charity, cook at camp, wherever you can help out and get noticed. Why? Because people *will notice,* they will like you, and will have nothing but glowing things to say about you to other people. And a lot of them will be guys, or know hot guys. **Being popular is never a bad thing.** "But what does all of this have to do with stringing a guy along?" Everything. If you are going to have the ability to string a guy along, you need to sink as many hooks in him as you can get. <u>Beauty is much more than your physical looks, or your willingness to show off parts of your body.</u> Beauty comes in *many forms* men are helplessly drawn to; but, of course, too many times men don't even consciously notice until it is too late.

We are so wrapped up "thinking" that your breasts, waist, and face are all that matters that we are sucker punched* by things like your perfume, a certain quality to your voice, a bracelet you are wearing, your smile, your attitude toward us, the way you move, (and so on). It truly is the little things that get you the most. Never underestimate the value of attention to detail when setting out your hooks to snag the attention of men.

* "Sucker punch." A cheap shot in a fight. Actually, to properly deliver a sucker punch, it is best not to be in a fight. Simply sneak up behind someone and *WHAM!* Hit them as hard as you can, and send them down fast. This is one of the most cowardly things a guy could do. But *as a term,* "sucker punch" rocks! Very descriptive of being taken by surprise, and laid out.

Examples of hooks

Angelina Jolie has consistently been voted one of the top "most attractive women in the world" by men. Why? Well, she is hotter than hell. **But there is so much more than that.** She has more hooks than that fisherman guy with the yellow suit on the fish sticks package in the frozen section of the grocery store.

Whether she knows them or not *is not important.* What is important is that YOU do. All of the following will attract *some* men. <u>Not all men will bite at the same hook.</u> Some men will be turned off by some of these hooks. Others will be mesmerized by them, unable to tear themselves away. Some men will nibble at one hook, while others will helplessly flop around like a fish out of water, making complete idiots of themselves because everything they see about her makes them excited about her femininity.

A small handful of
Angelina Jolie's hooks:

Her overall physical beauty on screen

Specifically: Her lips

Specifically: Her eyes

Specifically: Her voice

Her talent as an actress (this shows in the characters she plays)

The fact that she is a celebrity (it certainly doesn't hurt)

Her tireless efforts* to help the U.N. make this world a better place for people who are starving.

That blood/necklace thing**

(and so on . . .)

*"tireless efforts"—Angelina Jolie doesn't need to travel to the far corners of the world to save the planet. She can write a check and be done with it, like most people. She doesn't need to even do that to be popular, she's Angelina Jolie. How many other celebrity females (or men for that matter) do you see spending copious amounts of their own money and time trying to help make this world a nicer place? Out of all of those (I'm sure you have come up with a huge list), how many are getting themselves nominated for "humanitarian awards" so they sell more tickets? Angelina doesn't go around broadcasting her humanitarian activities. She just does it. *THAT is beyond sexy (to some men).*

**Whatever YOU think about her carrying around a bit of her boyfriend's blood in a necklace *means nothing* (sorry). What matters is that *to certain men,* <u>that says</u> she is sensual, exotic, erotic, LOYAL, and that the bond she had with that guy was the kind of bond every guy (who likes Angelina Jolie) <u>wishes he had</u> with her.

Blah, blah, blah . . . so it's great to be Angelina Jolie. Yeah, yeah. Now it's time to forget all about that avatar of Aphrodite, and focus on you. Now that you have some examples of what to look for, **what are your strengths?** What do you already (secretly or overtly) pride yourself in? What are the hooks that men will get tangled up in over you? Your eyes, your walk, your voice, the way you dress, your grace or even frumpiness, perhaps your casual attitude toward life—these are all things that draw men to you every day, when you show them to the world.

If you are a "Goth," then be a Goth and forget all of the idiots who are not attracted to your style and allow those who are to drive themselves insane with desire for you. The same premise holds true whether you are a tomboy, wallflower, gypsy, an activist, artist, performer, or caretaker by nature. No matter who or what you are inside, there is no shortage of attractive, passionate men who want to know more about you, and be part of the world you surround yourself with. Finding them is easier when you lay out your strong points and let them get snagged by one (or more).

Your hooks *naturally* attract the type of people you want in your life, people who desire the specific qualities and skills you possess. This makes life infinitely more fun than simply looking for someone who matches a few generic criteria. Your hooks bring to your life people who are personalized to your lifestyle choices rather than generic humans who leave you with a bland taste in your mouth after a few hours with them.

Identifying your personal hooks may not seem like an easy task at first, but you must stay with it. We all too easily notice our faults and flaws, and criticize those who seem "too aware" of their own strong points, but that will stop now. Your homework is to start looking closely at what makes you special, what you like about yourself, and what other people who like the same things as you will like about you as well. Take a few minutes each day to think of positive things about yourself and prioritize them as you discover more. We will break these down into major and minor hooks. The strength of your hook (like a hook in a song) will be how well you do it, and how well men respond to it. **Don't show these lists to anyone.** They are for your eyes only:

My major hooks are

_____

_____

_____

_____

_____

_____

_____

_____

My minor hooks are

_____

_____

_____

_____

_____

_____

_____

Okay, so hopefully you have spent some time thinking about what parts of your personality, body, and various talents and/or abilities you use to get men interested in "brand (your name here)." If you want to be able to have a vast collection of men to choose from (and why not—every woman deserves to feel good about herself), then you need to know what you've got and how, and when, to flaunt it.

The more a man thinks you can walk on water, the more crap he will put up with, hoops he will jump through, money he will spend on you, places he will take you, and years of his life he will devote to your happiness. Let me tell you, if you have never been worshiped, it is a pretty intoxicating sensation. Once you have your man hooked (like a fish), then you simply allow nature to take its course. He will start demanding more from you (because *it physically hurts him* to be away from you), and you, in turn, naturally blame circumstance. That old devil circumstance is a crotchety old bugger.

Play with him: Have fun, go places (alone with him, or in small groups, but NOT "double dates"), invite him over with friends for dinner, see him occasionally in quasi-romantic settings (like an action flick), but don't go too far romantically or become too much of a "buddy/pal."

You are keeping him as a (guy) friend, but you should be careful to not overtly classify the relationship you have with him. It will always be a balancing act, and it will be different with each guy, but you can do it. I have faith in you. With just a little practice, you will be able to do this in your sleep. Try not to break too many hearts.

You string him along by keeping him fed, but on a diet. Kinda like a fast. The trick is not to let him know that he is on a diet. Remember that *you* are not to blame. Circumstance is; but even if it was not, there is no guarantee that you will hook up with him. Give him attention, *and* appropriate affection, but keep circumstance up in front of you like a shield. Also let him know that while you are interested, it is not a simple matter of solving a problem "so that you two can be together."

Flirt, but flirt lightly. If he is at all interested, you will see it written all over him. If you think he is being coy and are thinking of teasing or testing him, *be careful of falling into his trap of feigned disinterest.* This is one of the few tricks that guys have to trap girls they want or like, and so it is vastly overused (and overrated). **Once they think you are interested, they will often fake disinterest to see if you try a little harder.** This is of the "treat her like crap once you have hooked her, because women everywhere just can't resist a challenge" school of thought. Obviously, you don't want this to happen to you if you are the one doing the stringing along.

How to get a guy to commit to you
*See also what I wrote about hooks and
about stringing guys along (above).*

There is a long-held belief that men are afraid of commitment, but the truth is that <u>guys commit to women every day</u>. In fact, guys *try to commit to women so much* that it makes a lot of women feel pressured and "creeped out." Men generally commit to women when they think that a certain woman is better than anything else they will find, or <u>when they are afraid that some other guy will steal her away</u>. You see, it is not that a guy won't commit to you. The problem is almost always that *the guy you want the most* won't commit to you.

There's nothing wrong with being picky. In fact, I advocate being extremely picky. How many times have you heard "don't settle for less" (usually from someone trying to sell you car insurance)? When you settle for less than you really want, you are stuck with what you get, and that is obviously not what you want. **As simple as this sounds**, it happens every day because far too many of you <u>make the mistake of settling for less than you secretly want</u>. Then you try to "change the guy," to make him more palatable to your tastes, which makes him rebel against "you trying to control him." That leads to him complaining about it to his friends and everyone ends up unhappy. *Stop it! Stop—it! Stop, stop, stop!*

Now that you know how to get men to do anything you want (You have read the whole book, right? *Twice?*) and you know <u>how to find the type of guys you want</u>—you know how to make them come say hello, *and what you should do if they are too stupid to approach you*—**why accept less than what you *really* want?**

Make sure that you are using every trick you have learned here and everything you knew before you read any of this. The simplest way to get a guy to commit—*to you*—is to make him happy to have you in his life, without making yourself miserable in the process. Remember that everything in life is conditional on some level.

Think of why you would commit to anyone you find attractive. *They make you feel good about yourself.* They are always happy to see you, make you feel sexy, treat you well, but the most important thing is that you feel empowered when you are around them. You feel on top of the world, like you can do or be any-thing, and that is a very addictive feeling. So, *be an addiction* (with lots of spiky "hooks").

You are now as addictive as crack cocaine. You are crack cocaine with a funny hat and spiky hooks. You are such a potent intoxicant that men stop what they are doing whenever you are around, and look for ways to impress or please you. You are now irresistible to men—right? If you answered "no," you need to go back through this book and stop "reading," *and start "doing." But . . . before you do your best to get some guy to commit to you, be absolutely sure that THIS is what you want.* See: "The List," and "The Other List." It makes no sense to get a guy to commit to you, *and then* find out he is a total loser. Let women who have not read this book do that.

How to get a guy to break up with you—and think it was his idea

Obviously, this is easier with some guys than it is with others. These are the same tricks guys use to get you to break things off with them, so they can go after your best friend. So, if you suspect a guy doing this to you, *start drinking heavily.*

Stop wearing makeup around him. Stop dressing sexy for at least one month. Don't take chances by dressing sexy when he is away. Someone will have a camera and plaster your pretty face all over MySpace, and then where will you be? He will find out, and get jealous, and then start accusing you of all sorts of crap. Just dress down. This works instantly, and the more you do it daily, the more powerul the cumulative effect will be.

Be a boring girlfriend. Introduce him to your hot friends. This means making a friend who is hot and going out with both of them, leaving them alone for a moment while you go to the bathroom, get a drink (whatever), and let him do the wrong thing. Don't bother catching him. Whether she is interested in him or not doesn't matter. What you want is for him to start hitting on girls when you are "not around."

Be uninterested in his hobbies or passions. Ask him why he is so obsessed with these particular acivities, rather than some other activity (pick something other men do that he doesn't). Start dragging him to the ballet, opera, or any other decidedly non-masculine place of entertainment. Always be too tired for sex, and be mildly non-committal when he is affectionate ("Oops! I have gum in my mouth. I have to spit it out before I kiss you," or "Ow! It's okay, you pulled my hair. Ow! You did it again. It's okay . . . ow!").

Finally, "withholding" works better than anything else you can think up. When you withhold affection and attention from a guy, you remove any desire he has to make you happy. In fact, if you do it really well, you can effectively destroy his will to live. If you are tired of a guy, and you need him to go, move on with your life and send clear signals that he is not a part of it. These techniques will drive a subtle wedge between you and any guy. The more high maintenance, and "not-very-fun" you are, the more you eat away at any bond a guy has with you. Sometimes all it takes is a weekend.

How to get a certain type of guy
(executive, fireman, celebrity . . .)

If you absolutely know what kind of men you want to have in your life on a regular basis, your chances of getting them interested in you are much better than randomly bumping into someone who will sweep you off your feet. This is why you filled out your lists of wants and _don't_ wants earlier in the book. If you have filled in your lists and at the top words like Doctor, Artist, Pilot, Fireman, or Professional Musician appear, then it's time to go fishing where the fish are. Forget the generic places to meet guys, and find excuses to be at the places where they congregate exclusively. Use your appeal to get attention, and if that doesn't work fast enough for you, use the techniques in this book to get guys to talk to you. The fact that you are where they are on a regular basis makes it much easier for them to approach you.

How to see beyond his pretty words
when you first meet a guy

When you first meet a guy, many of your friends (especially the guys) can instantly see through him. If you happen to have one handy, have him watch and let you know what he thinks. Make sure that the friend you enlist doesn't secretly want you (or the other guy), or he may "flavor" his assessment of the other guy with his secret desire(s). But what if you don't have a friend handy to get a second opinion. Here are a few ways you can spot someone who is playing you:

Generally the smoother he is, the more of a professional he is. When a guy *first approaches you*—and during the first 5 minutes—if you get the sense that everything he says comes across as if he has known you for years, you might have a pro on your hands. Have fun, but try to trip him up conversationally here and there to see whether he flounders, or if he rolls over every conversational bump like he has practiced this before—on hundreds of women.

Don't outright accuse him of being a player, as that would spoil the fun of trapping him with his own words. Ask him questions based on the things he is telling you, that make him reveal things that may not make him look so "hot." A real pro will field these questions easily, and turn them back on you so fast that you will find yourself on the defensive, and for some strange reason *wondering if you are all that hot yourself.* Beware of him playing the "humble guy" approach, trying to elicit feelings of empathy and compassion from you. Any other guy will find himself stumbling around a bit while he tries to regain his composure. After all, he is trying to impress you—so let him (try).

Also: Watch how fast he goes for the touch. <u>Touch is essential in seduction.</u> How soon, and where he touches you will usually tell you his intentions, and how hot he thinks you are. There are occasional exceptions (he was drunk and bumped into you by mistake), but if he is offering you "a back rub" within 10 minutes of meeting you, expect to lose your bra within the hour. Most men aren't "dogs" as much as they simply are starved for attention, unaware of how counterintuitive their actions are to getting what they really want, and the moment they get some of yours, they usually go a little overboard. Worst of all, they have to show off in front of their friends. It has always been like this. <u>The ones you have to watch out for the most</u> are the men *who aren't starved for attention.* They have an arsenal of tricks up their sleeves (both of them—be sure to check), and know how to manipulate you through their words, logic, promises, and occasional gifts.

Most men will try to impress you at some point. That is simply how they are made. Watch out for the ones that boastfully show off how wealthy, powerful, or talented they are. This is not just meant to impress you, it is also designed to intimidate you. If that is what you want, and you know that you are being seduced, *enjoy the ride.* But don't think for a moment that men are automatically pro-grammed to "give you stuff" (especially expensive things) just because you are "you." When a man gives you something he usually doesn't "expect" something (except in cases where he is seriously disturbed). *He "hopes"* that you will appreciate what he has sacrificed for you, and that you will like him enough to share your time and emotions (and body) with him.

EXPECTATION is completely different from <u>trying to impress you enough to build interest in him,</u> so that you will end up WANTING to share yourself with him. Don't confuse the two, or you will just end up missing out on a lot of fun—and probably end up with the wrong men anyway.

One more time—only because this one point is the source of MOST of the problems too many women have with men—and men have with you:

A sales girl at Macy's will try to impress upon you the differences in each perfume you try. You already know that you want perfume, but rather than just grab the cheapest one *(never a good idea when deciding perfume—or men),* she will help you see why a certain brand is more to your tastes than another. Guys are just like that. Except this is like the perfumes trying to sell themselves to you. They are all clamoring, *"Try me on, you will like me."*

There's no better feeling in the world than being so sought after that someone is trying to show you why what they have will make you happier. YOU become the center of their world at that moment.

144

This puts YOU in control, because YOU get to say "yes." Anyone can say "no" (and once you have convinced anyone that you mean "no," you lose your power over them), but *the possibility* of you actually saying "yes" at some point drives people to help you get to the places you want to be.

What to do/say when his girlfriend/wife shows up and accuses you of trying to steal her man

Oh crap! You hit it off with this cute guy and are having a nice little conversation and, naturally, he has said *nothing at all* about having a wife, and then suddenly Xena the Warrior Princess shows up and starts a scene. She takes one look at you and decides that her man can't be trusted to talk to you. What she is really saying is that her man can't be trusted. Hmmm . . . maybe she should have bought a copy of this book *before* she started dating him. How the hell should I know what to do? I am a guy! Guys are dumb. We like cat fights, or at least <u>the fantasy</u> of a good cat fight. Did you bring an extra set of clothes to wear after you two shred each other's blouses (like in a beer commercial)? Maybe you could ask her if she wants to make out. *Now THAT would be sexy.*

What to do/say when his BOYFRIEND shows up and accuses you of trying to steal his man

You're kidding—right? You have been having a nice little conversation with this hot guy, and he is gay? Damn. Sucks to be you. Tell yourself that he wasn't that hot anyway.

How to get him to ask for your phone number

He's not getting the hint . . . Try this: Tell him that you are running late for something. Tell him that you would like to continue this conversation later (assuming you two have actually been talking about anything interesting). Say that you have a book you would like to recommend, but you can't remember the title off hand. Or casually mention something happening next Friday, and say that you think he might have a good time there. If he doesn't get the hint by now, you will have to ask him *for his number.*

How to get his phone number

Tell him that you are running late for _____, and that you enjoyed meeting him. Shake his hand (if it looks clean), and ask him if he has a card. If he doesn't, fish around your purse for a pen and have him write it down. Ask him what is a good time to reach him. *(Is it a home, work, or cell number?)* Thank him and scoot! Let him worry about whether you will ever call him.

How to get his phone number
— as a friend —

Tell him that you are running late for _____, and that you enjoyed meeting him. Shake his hand (if it looks clean), and ask him if he has a card. If he doesn't, fish around your purse for a pen and have him write it down. Tell him that there is something (obviously platonic, like a lecture) happening on (pick a day of the week), and you will call with details to see if he wants to "tag along." Remember to smile and be friendly. The subtle "friend" indications will be glaringly obvious to all but the most smitten guys.

(more) fun facts!
(about men):

The "right woman" can drive any man mad with passion (or just insane), inspire him to throw his life down for her, throw it away (also for her), get him to build monuments that defy time, write, paint, or chisel in stone masterpieces that also defy time, lose his hair, lose 20 pounds, change his religion, and yes, even inspire him to stop hogging the covers and (gently) lower the seat when he is finished. How does this miracle worker accomplish these amazing feats? Seduction. She is *more woman* than any other girl he meets. By her attire, grace, smile, glance, and her kindness to him, she holds him close to her, his attention, and his future.

Seduction is not about sex. *(Try telling the average man-on-the-street that.)* Seduction is all about bonding; dissolving willpower. It's the art of clouding the mind, mesmerizing someone with your strongest points, and creating a fantasy that they can step into for a time. Seduction makes dreams come true.

fun facts!
(about you):

You can be that woman (see above). In fact, *you already are that girl*—for men all over the world. Now I wonder, how will you go about getting them to find you?

fun facts!
(about that bitch he used to date):

If she had *any real power* over his thought process, it was because she let the various parts of her femininity do all of the hard work for her. She appealed to his biological urges (sex, love, compassion, and/or comfort level) and made herself the obvious choice for these things to him. After that, his willpower stood no chance. To break her spell, you just have to appeal to him on more levels, or more deeply on the same levels. You have all the tools you need already—you simply have to use them.

The anatomy of a pick-up line

. . . and people wonder what I could possibly have against pick-up lines. Pick-up lines are best when they are used as a joke, or when you just feel superficial. Because there is a pervasive stigma that *"guys will say anything to get laid,"* including using a pick-up line to meet women, when a woman uses a pick-up line on a man, it usually becomes fun and funny.

How to deal with all of the attention you will be getting from men
*without going insane, losing yourself in the process,
or coming across as a "pampered bitch"*

An interesting thing about fame . . . Once we get it, it rarely turns out to be exactly what we hoped it would be. Being popular is fun, until you realize that you can't usually choose exactly who will like you the most. You will find that people who you desire will have nothing to do with you (for reasons of their own); others will smile politely at you while wishing you a horrible death; and still others (whom you would be afraid to meet in a dark alley) will flock to you as if you were their messiah.

Face it: <u>Popularity sucks</u>! Everyone you meet wants something from you, even if it's just your approval, acceptance, or time. *Your desires* become secondary to your public. If you are going to be popular, you have to understand the rules.

Contract
with your public

You are allowed privacy, and "private time," but only in ways that do not infringe on the rights of your public to reach out to you. It is impossible to be popular, and simultaneously be a hermit. And forget "quality time with the ones you love." That will have to take a back seat as well, unless you can balance your time spent with your closest friends with your time spent with your most important friends (your public). Also: Your public is your friend collectively, and therefore each member of your public is your friend individually. You are not required to know (or remember) their names, but don't you dare come across as aloof, nor uncaring of their appreciation and/or affection for you, unless you are tired of being "liked," and "popular." Nothing turns people away from a celebrity like insincerity, or a lack of compassion from the "popular person."

Sign here: X _____

Think of meeting *your favorite* celebrity. How would you want them to respond to you? Would you want them to glance at you as if you were gum stuck to their shoe? Or . . . what if they smiled, listened to you blather on mindlessly for a moment or two, telling them how much you loved _____, and then they casually invited you to enjoy a cup of coffee with them before they flew off to Paris? (Unless you met them *in Paris*, in which case they would be flying off to Sydney.)

Handling yourself in public is crucial to becoming, and staying, popular. But your private moments are where *you exist*, where you become what you are popular *for being*. Once you become popular, you must never stop *actually doing* what it is that made you popular, hence the time-honored Hollywood phrase, "You are only as good as your last project." Center yourself by building your schedule around your passions. The majority of your time should be doing what it is that makes you popular—but remember that *this is what you enjoy doing whether anyone else cares or not.* From there, allocate time spent doing *other things* you enjoy, but that have nothing to do with what "pays the rent," so to speak. Finally, allow time to be eaten up in case you run into someone who wants "some of your time." This allows you to give them some without the pressure of eating into someone else's (or your) time. The result is that everyone wins (especially you).

You see, it is not easy staying popular, but it can be handled without too much effort once you establish a healthy routine. *The rewards are obvious.* Remember to be sincerely gracious at all times, <u>especially when you are under pressure, running late, and the times you are being harassed by jerks</u>. This may not always be possible, but the more often you can be gracious, the more forgiving your most important friends will be.

Keeping your story straight

Honesty is more than "the best policy." Honesty works. It is harsh, brutal, and not very often pretty, but if you build a reputation for honesty, you can demand it in return at any time from anyone, and you will command more respect than just about anyone you know. More important: you will find people running to your defense when there is ever any doubt of your character.

149

Now that's all fine and dandy, <u>but for those times</u> *when you just have to lie*, it is important that you learn how to keep your story intact, even under the closest scrutiny. You see, I am something of a realist. Honesty is nice in a fairy-tale version of reality, but I don't disillusion myself by expecting it from everyone, 100% of the time. I wouldn't advise you becoming too reliant on the expectation of honesty from random guys you meet. When fabricating a story to a guy, your primary concern should be that he will look for holes in your story based on his emotional opinion about you, and the condition of his libido. Anything that affects his ability to get attention from you, or *(his perception of)* your penchant for giving your affections to someone *other than him,* will be dwelt upon first.

It's best to avoid giving details if possible, as most guys care more about results (affection from you) than they will ever care about details. Guys are notorious for being oblivious to details, preferring to see the end results of our efforts. Our jobs continually reinforce this mentality in us: Work, work, work . . . get paid! All we want is the money, but we have to work so we can get the money—so we work *and we forget about work* <u>once we have the money</u>. Who needs details? Beware of the occasional guy you meet who nitpicks you about details. He is probably a control freak who will do his best to make your life miserable if you get involved with him. Even if he isn't, do you really want to be nagged all of the time by an insecure guy who feels the need to correct you, as if you were a child? This need to correct is in reality a need to perfect his world by perfecting everything and everyone around him. It comes from a loving mentality, if you consider loving someone to be trying to fix them by showing them how they are wrong on a regular basis. It is best to leave these guys for someone with masochistic tendencies.

Quickie #8:
Details, details . . .

Hey! You know those little things in life called details? I am certain that you have seen these before: They include issues like "whether we will call you back" *(here's a hint: if we like you, we won't <u>stop</u> calling you)*, the fact that we left the cap off of the toothpaste (again), that the kids have nothing in the house to eat but pizza, ice cream, and chocolate ("good food"—lucky bastards), while we sit around watching the game. You know . . . *details.*

Guess what? **We don't care.** Don't bother us with "details." They make you look less attractive to us. Our mistress doesn't nag us about the dishes, the kids, or the toothpaste (not that we . . . er . . . have a mistress, of course). But that is not the issue. The issue is that *we–just–don't–care.* We are too wrapped up in some other thought process, and nagging us just makes you look bad. It doesn't solve the problem any more than it makes us care. I know that details make the world go around, but **we get enough of that "devil in the details" at work every day.** *You probably do too.*

So how is it making us like you any more by complaining to us about details? I'm not saying it's fair. *Of course* it's not fair! But this isn't a book about being fair, it's a book about getting what *you want done* in a very unfair world. So handle the details *and give us the results*—or be creative in presenting us with the details. Find ways to make us like you for them. Try using what you learn in this book. We will all be happier because of your ability to get things done.

Helpful advice that will make you look better, sexier, and more fun than other girls

Be versatile! Guys *love women* who don't take 45 minutes to get ready to go somewhere. Guys are constantly being held up by women for various reasons, so be the exception *(they will notice).* You can even mention it casually to see how often men you know are held up waiting for other women to "get ready."

Don't bother explaining to us what a hassle it is to get ready: We-just–don't–care. It is better to just be ready to go (most places) on a moment's notice, and watch how much easier the men in your life are to deal with. You can always "stop along the way and grab something." Generally guys are much more okay with that *than waiting to actually start* going somewhere.

Plan ahead and have a bag of essentials packed for an overnight stay, or an instant weekend getaway. Just grab a bag and cram everything you might need over a 24- or 48-hour period and toss the whole thing in your closet—or better yet, the trunk of your car. You will always be ready for anything.

Pack light. If your guy sees you hauling out a fifty-pound suitcase when he springs a "weekend in Vegas" on you Friday night, he will be both suspicious and annoyed. Lingerie, bikini, toothpaste—just the basics. Buy whatever else you need on the road. By planning ahead and packing accordingly, you will come across as "free, fun, and adventurous" to guys you like, instead of "a typical woman" who has to pack everything she owns—*once she finally makes up her mind* on whether or not she is going along. This is not a reasonable assessemnt of women. It is a pervasive one though. I realize this is not even remotely fair. *But this book is not about playing fair, or making the world "fair," nor is this book about levelling the playing field.* **This book is about <u>you</u> finally getting what <u>you</u> want from life before <u>you</u> finally give up on your <u>dreams.</u>** This book is about playing to men's innate weaknesses and getting them to WANT to do stuff for you. *Face it:*

Men, the world over, will continue to do stupid things for women on a regular basis—*with or without your help*—so you might as well guide them along. This keeps them out of trouble (hopefully), it is fun for both of you, *and* it can get you a mountain of "free stuff." Most men have such low expectations of women (based on their experiences with women prior to meeting you) that even a little spontaneity will make you look *infinitely more fun* than other girls—<u>even if you have nothing else going for you</u> (which I highly doubt). Let other girls sit at home waiting for the phone to ring. YOU will be the one invited everywhere, and getting as much attention as you can possibly stand . . . *but just in case that fails . . .*

Here are a few things you can do <u>RIGHT NOW</u> to make yourself more beautiful to ANY man!

Find your own *personal* style! The guys who like <u>that</u>, will <u>love</u> you! After all, this is YOUR life—have some fun with it. Always remember, you are automatically twice as sexy when you are doing something <u>you are passionate about</u>. This has the added benefit of attracting the men *you want to meet* while subtly pushing away the ones who don't even like the things that are important to you. But, if you are not picky at the moment, and just want to have some fun getting attention from hot guys . . .

Get him drunk!

Laugh at his jokes.

Have a few
drinks yourself.

(a few)

Smile *(at him)*. This actually works better than alcohol, and it is free. When you smile sincerely at the person you are meeting, especially if it is a man, you are sending a message of welcome and inviting that person to relax and drop their defenses a bit. A truly winning smile isn't about dazzling teeth, or a movie star complexion. It is about making the other person believe that *you* are smiling at *them,* and not just putting on a smile like a mask.

Chase away any other girls in the area.

Touch him casually, and often. This will tell you instantly how he feels about you, and if his opinion of you changes, your touch will evoke reactions from him that tell you instantly where you two stand, even if he doesn't realize that he is sending these signals so clearly. Touching people who we are not imtimately familair with is such a taboo these days that we have all become starved for casual, friendly, intimate physical contact. This makes the power of your touch ten times more powerful than it would be if we weren't all running around afraid of touching other people. People need touch. *We all crave it,* but we have so many safeguards and rituals established about touching each other that we end up starving ourselves for attention and compressing the focus of our need for touch into sex. This removes the casual fun of sex and makes it responsible for most of the sensual enjoyment our psyches need to stay healthy. By touching people casually, and subtly, you stimulate a bond with them on an emotional level they rarely experience. Use the power of your touch (selectively) to determine the interest and motives of the men in your life, and to empower those bonds you want to develop.

Use a "cute pet" as a prop to break the ice . . .

Get him to pet
"your pet."

Wear less. *(Not "nothing," just "less." Be creative.)*

Speak less: <u>Get him to work *to impress you*</u>. Popularity coaches have been telling us for years that people love the sound of their own names more than they love just about anything else in conversation. More important, however, is that **we like to tell other people our opinions and experiences** and we want them to validate us by agreeing, or at least sympathizing with our plight. Even though it is much more fun to tell other people about ourselves, *the real power* is in getting *them* to talk about themselves, or what is important to them, in such a way that they start to like us for *listening*.

Talk about things
he is interested in.

This little trick works so well it is downright unfair to other women. It makes the man you are talking to think you are somehow different, special, and a cut above other women who are only interested in what he can do for them.

155

Comfort zones
versus
motivation

How much he does for you compared to
how much you have to do to get him to do it

Stomp!

Stomp!

He's way out of control.
It's time to find a better man.

Is it really worth
this much effort?

You have to negotiate to get just about
anything you want; but, for the most
part, you get your needs met.

There's a lot of give and take.
This feels really healthy—
and it's kinda fun!

What a prince!
He's always thinking of you!

He's <u>always</u> thinking of you. No, really.
It's getting really creepy, like you are
being stalked, or corralled like a horse.

A man can (and usually will) fluctuate between zones.
Left on his own, the average man will move this way over time.

Are you worth "two month's salary"?
The absolute power of grace, sophistication, and charm

When all is said and done, it all comes down to this (. . . and the part about making elitism sexy). <u>Your physical beauty</u>, being the sum total of your looks, wardrobe (including accessories and your choice of perfume), your style, grace, charm, and attitude towards men—even towards life—multiplied by your passions, and *your ability to freely express your passion daily in your life*, <u>will decide the men you attract</u>. That's quite an equation.

If you want your life to be one of opulence and luxury, it helps to *re-create yourself as an object of opulence and luxury*—daily. Cinderella didn't win her prince because she was an uptight bitch. She was the epitome of femininity, and even through rags, a man can see that (whether he is a prince, or not). In this book, you will find all kinds of methods by which you can endear men to your way of thinking. But don't stop there. Read Dale Carnegie's *How to Win Friends and Influence People*. It is a bit dated, but it has sold over 15 million copies, so the old boy had to be right about something.

Practice your femininity on everyone. Be demure, polite, and friendly, but also watch people carefully, noting who would take advantage of your *perceived* naïveté. No matter your financial status, you can easily place yourself in the company of wealthy men. Your task from there is to get noticed by the men, without making it obvious to the women in the area that you are looking for attention from men. Grace, sophistication, and charm are sadly lacking in our populace today. These are the personality traits that will make you stand out, even if you only have a little of each to begin with. The more sincere you can be in your projection of these qualities, the more wealthy men will want to do things for you.

Above all else, never forget that by breaking the ice for a busy (or hesitant) man you <u>want</u> to meet, you are opening the doors to your future. ***You only need one "right guy" to say hello to.*** With all of the tools you have at your disposal now, you should not have to say hello to too many frogs on your way to landing your prince of a guy. If you have put to use any of what you have learned in this book—why would you settle for anything less?

How to make elitism sexy

Elitism is a double-edged sword. Pull it off properly and before you know it, you are flown to exotic locations on private jets. Do it wrong and you just look like an uptight bitch. Not to worry though, as I am *the undisputed king* of elitist bastards, I will show you how to make elitism work for you in just 3 easy steps! It's up to you to practice, but that is why God made so many jerks to hit on you. No sense wasting nice guys while you are sharpening your skills, as *nice guys* make *nice friends* who will buy you lots of *nice things* over time. So with all of that out of the way, let's get down to business, shall we?

How elitism works: Properly done, elitism simply says to other people, "I am better than you." You, of course, never use these words. To do so would be gauche. Also, never confuse *"I am better than you"* with *"I am more important than you,"* because in the greater scheme of things, not one of us is more important than any other (productive) member of society. This is where most women screw this up, so we will start by correcting that problem immediately. I hope I don't have to remind you, but just in case: Do not try to teach this to your friends. *The whole purpose of elitism is to shut out the riffraff, not to create a club that anyone can join.* Let your friends figure this out on their own.

If you really like them, show them how gracious and thoughtful you are **by buying them their own copy of this book.** *Naturally you will be using money you "borrowed" from a guy "friend" who is well-trained to give you things upon request* (never demand—it disembowels a man, and that leads to resentment, which leads to all sorts of trouble).

So, *"I am better than you."* Please allow me to provide you with an allegory to consider. Hopefully, this will help you permanently implant the sheer power of this attitude in your head. You are a tiger in the jungle. Actually, you would be a tigress, but that doesn't matter at the moment. What matters is that you are bright orange and have stripes. You are soft to the touch, hypnotically graceful, intoxicatingly beautiful, and so deadly that on a whim, you could have any man of your choice for dinner.

So in the jungle, you are naturally at the top of the food chain. You do what pleases you, when you desire to be pleased. You are a rare breed, as the jungle only supports a few tigers for every hundred or so giraffes, monkeys, and aardvarks. You are not *more important* than any other animal, because without the other animals frolicking happily in the jungle, <u>you would have to actually hunt</u> a tasty snack, instead of having them all but delivered to you whenever you are hungry. You see it takes all types to make a jungle.

But you are "better" than them in ways that are obvious to the most casual observer. A tiger (or tigress) builds its muscles to incredible mass by stretching them daily. Your workouts look like play to the other animals, but that is the nature of being "above and beyond" the norm. You are used to being misunderstood by inferior minds, so you smile graciously when confronted, and have pity on those who are more commonplace than you.

You should recognize this look on the face of any number of successful "supermodels" who have to deal with the inane questions and comments of the masses every day. Every time they are told by some man obsessed with them "how beautiful they are," it is just a reminder to them of why they spend so much time working on looking that good. Smile graciously and let the commoner pass, feeling like they have touched divinity.

The key to pulling off elitism (so that rich guys will fawn all over you, spending hundreds of thousands of dollars on you in an attempt to win your attention) is finesse. Much like tennis, it's all in the wrist. Remembering that you are the tigress of the jungle, you do not have to prove anything to anyone. Holding that picture of yourself in your head, gaze out politely at all of your subordinates in life and see them at your disposal. They all have their place and purpose, but you (for reasons only you know) are simply more gifted than them. They can choose to please you, or get out of your way in life, as pleases them. No matter. All that matters is that you maintain your poise while you seek out others like you.

Contrary to popularly held (mis)belief, elitism is not a product of wealth, power, or opulence. *Elitism draws these things to you* like flies to honey in the warm summer sun. Let those who have spent a lifetime gathering these tools of seduction (money, power, fame, luxury . . .) attempt to woo you with them. *You* need nothing *but attitude, and a resolute self-image* to be an elitist. You were born *naturally deserving of the finer things (and people) in life.* Start today by raising your standards, and do not let anyone tear you down. A true elitist would starve before she ever "ate crow."

Remember: You **resonate** elitism; not project it. It runs through your blood, and naturally oozes out *quietly,* regally. **It is not a sign you hold up.** It is something the quick catch, the wise are intrigued by, and the foolish throw money at. Think "hanger's on," that is wealth groupies; people who cannot help themselves, but to idolize the rich, in the hopes of joining their club one day. A little *quality* practice and you should be able to have people thinking you a celebrity (and racing to attend to your needs and desires) rather than a stuck-up bitch, in no time. The rewards are worth more than anything I could ever describe to you here.

Get a bucket of popcorn, a handful of musky scented candles, and rent the movie *The Hunger* (David Bowie, Catherine Deneuve, and Susan Sarandon). I believe it was made in the 1980s, so you may have to get it through Netflix, or search around a bit. Not only is it a *tres cool* cultish movie about vampires, but it is incredibly sexy in a way that elitists understand innately. Pay special attention to the club scene, with Bauhaus in the background, the casual nature the ankhs are "dealt with" absently, after they have served their use, and the seduction of Susan Sarandon. The movie reeks elitism without pretension. It also serves as a good lesson as to what can happen when you try to "let people into your exclusive club."

Unfortunately, you either "get it"—or you do not. If the movie is just too dry (like a Martini) for you, you may not be elitist material, which is not a bad thing at all. This movie is a good primer for elitism—to see if this reclusive world is right for you.

So . . . after all of this, let's say (just for fun) that you have found your true home. Suddenly you realize *why you have never felt comfortable* when you are surrounded by crowds of strangers. You have had a revelation as to why diamonds *only* come from Tiffany & Co., coffee only from the Blue Mountain of Jamaica (as if it came from anywhere else), and why you always run in small circles of friends. You are not a snob. Far from it: You do your best to be polite, friendly, and as outgoing as possible, considering that you really do not like dealing with people when you don't have to. You my friend, just might be an elitist. If so, then it is time to learn how to use your secret superpowers to your advantage in life.

Above all, always be polite—especially when you are dealing with *obvious inferiors.* Other people are watching your interactions, and their casual observations of you are what will decide whether you are held in high esteem or thought of as a snob. Your appeal lies in the fact that you exude charm and grace, but hold a poise and sophistication that transcends whatever situation you find yourself in. Your inner image of yourself *carries the weight for you.*

This is what they used to teach in charm school, but charm school is as dead as the dodo bird. I cannot force myself to be any more obvious than to hint that one might just be able to create a small fortune teaching future generations of women to "be charming." Take it as you will.

This is the attitude that draws people to you. Once you find someone who catches your eye, don't rush over to them and gush all over them. Smile (mildly) seductively and *approach them.* This puts you in the alpha position. If you wait for them to approach you, you lose the element of control.

Introduce yourself, and ask a question that relates to them. If you can ask them how they are enjoying their day, the party (assuming you are at one), the scenery, et al., so much the better. The psychology here is an elevated state of mind, asking (politely) from a lofty place how they are doing. It sends a signal of *"I am—are you?"* without being too obvious. If you were mistaken, you have not shown your cards and can smile politely and move on to more sophisticated prospects.

When you are certain that you have found a new playtoy, it is time to allow the other person to cross the threshold of your psychological tower. Invite them as an equal by being sincerely interested in what they have to say, yet slightly reserved, *preferring to ask them questions* (usually asking them to clarify what they are saying, but vary your approach in how you ask, so as not to come across like a parrot) *than rambling on and on about your own beliefs.* "Elitists inquire. They do not state the obvious."

161

Not only does this give you the advantage of finding out more about *them* while figuring out if you have enough interest in them to allow them to continue taking up your time, but a mouth kept shut leaks no fopahs.

It is far easier to allow people to create a fantasy of you as being some regal goddess by letting them blather on—while you respond inquisitively, occasionally—than it is to impress them with your own opinion. It is a strange thing that *we feel more attracted to people who know us* than we do to people we know. Always keep that in mind when influencing men. *Perhaps we are all a bit* narcissistic, needing to be "understood," and "appreciated," so that we can truly love ourselves. This is the power of elitism. If you can get others to see you as friendly, special*, and possibly even otherworldly, but quietly reserved, you will find people going out of their way to impress you. Once you have a little firsthand experience with this, you will see how easy it is to get guys to do backflips for you without you having to say a word.

*("special") You have any number of inherent qualities of personality and talents at your disposal. Collectively, these things make you, "you." Pick a few that you like and hold them close. Rest your sense of identity and self-worth on these when you are in self-doubt. Remember these wonderful things about yourself, things that no one can take away from you, whenever you are faced with a crowd of strange faces. Smile gracefully and remember that you are the tigress. That will help instill the confidence you need to deal with the rabble.

Invite your favorite playtoys along on some of your milder adventures, and definitely the ones where you are absolutely certain that they cannot make it. By allowing them to catch glimpses of your exclusivity, you are planting seeds of appearance to germinate in their own fertile imaginations. When these seeds take root, they will blossom into opinions of you based on the image you want them to hold. Your goal here is to come across as an extremely fun companion with more class and character than finances (at the moment). This all but invites them to correct this imbalance by using their wealth to impress you—and isn't that nice?

It happens every day, all over the world. It could happen to you.

Dealing with obsession
His . . . yours . . . your ex's

Obsession: *(noun)* ob·ses·sion

1. Compulsive preoccupation with a fixed idea or an unwanted feeling or emotion, often accompanied by symptoms of anxiety.

2. A compulsive, often unreasonable idea or emotion.

Obsession is a powerful emotion. It makes all things possible, or drives you insane trying to get there. Obsession can be sexy or scary, depending on *who* is obsessing on *what*. I was going to write a long section on how to deal with obsession, but really what it comes down to is this:

If you have problems due to your obsession over someone— get help. Don't be embarrassed. **It is far better to be embarrassed for a few minutes** out of your life than it is to be hauled into court as a stalker, or end up cutting yourself. We all get obsessed with something or someone at some point in our lives. E-v-e-r-y-o-n-e does. *So, you are not alone in this at all.* Sometimes this is healthy, other times it is not. If yours is "not" at the moment, just get help. **Then come back out and play.**

If you are having trouble with your boyfriend's, husband's, ex's (you get the idea) obsessive tendencies, then you need to call the police. Their number is nine-one-one. Don't become a Nicole Brown. Okay . . . let's get back to something fun.

Reasons you should have
a lot of guy "friends"

You never know when you'll need:

👍 A ride home at 2 a.m.

👍 $20.

👍 $20 to buy another copy of this book _because you actually
believed_ that your girlfriend who asked to borrow _this copy_
was going to give it back.

👍 A ride home at 2 a.m. after your guy "friend" got sloppy
drunk and professed his undying love to you _(and, of course,
he drove you to the party)._

👍 A shoulder to cry on.

👍 Someone <u>safe</u> to have comfort sex with (and a shoulder to
cry on) when your boyfriend sleeps with your best friend.

👍 $100.

👍 Some jerk beat up for harassing you.

👍 $1,000.

👍 A date for your best friend _(not the one who slept with your
boyfriend, your "new" best friend)._

Your male "friends" are those wonderful men who will go out to
coffee with you and let you gossip happily about anyone, go club-
bing with you when you can't find one of your girlfriends to drag
along, patiently listen as you complain to them about your "jerk"
boyfriend(s), and even let you spend the night, sleeping next to
them in their bed when you are too drunk to drive home—and
never "try anything."

Oh god, I think I'm going to vomit.

Guy "friends" come in different varieties depending on their personality, their level of interest in you (as a friend), their level of interest in you (how badly they want to tie you up and have sex with you), their attractiveness, and proximity to you.

One thing that all of your guy "friends" have in common is that they are genuinely happy to see you, *which means that they like your personality and who you are as a person.* This is the kind of validation and acceptance that you will rarely get on an ongoing basis from a boyfriend.

Your guy "friends" offer you a certain mildly-conditional form of male attention that can often smooth out the rough spots in life.

This little bit of extra male attention can make life supremely enjoyable (e.g., they really like *you*) or supremely frustrating (they *really* like you). When choosing a guy "friend," it is important to discern the quality of the guy before making too deep of a commitment of trust and time. The right "friend" will be there for you whenever you need, while the wrong one(s) will be waiting for their chance to have sex with you when you are too drunk to care. Just because a guy is friendly (to you) *does not make him your "friend."* The sooner you learn this, the less hassle the guys in your life will be. Your (true) guy "friends" will have any number of reasons for liking you, but they generally fall into these categories:

They think you are attractive. This is a compliment. It just means that you are doing your job right. You are attracting men who like how you look, *but also like who you are.* Who cares if they want to have sex with you? That is part of being a guy.

They are emotionally attracted to you. This is even better (as long as this doesn't get out of hand). This means that in your daily life, you are allowing people to see your personality without pretension. The problem with having guys as friends who have a crush on you is that *they are experiencing real emotions* of unknown depth. When you hook up with various guys, or you get engaged (and so on), they will be visibly affected.

If you have chosen your friends carefully, they will support you emotionally, and perhaps even financially as well. But, if you let an obsessive guy slip past your defenses and become a "friend," you will more than likely be in for some heavy drama. These situations are far too common, and only you can stop this from happening in your own life. So always choose your friends wisely.

They think you are *cool*, and they have common interests with you. This is the absolute best. When you get one of these guys in your life, do what you can to keep the friendship solid, and strong. These kinds of friendships are rare, but even if they were commonplace, they would be worth more than gold. These friendships make life fun, hard times bearable, and the best times even better.

Friendship is truly the magic of life *(even at a sub-atomic level, but that is a puzzle that molecular physicists will "eventually" discover—remember you heard it here first!)*. The very best guys make incredibly loyal friends. Most guys like having a few cool women to hang out with. It is a breath of fresh air to be able to hang out with a girl and not have to try to decipher her mood swings, fascination with gossip, or what it is about jerks, "bad boys," and complete idiots that turn her on so much.

It also gives us a chance to rant about girls in general, and find out what makes them do the strange things you do. Even if our "cool chick" friend has no answers, just being able to say certain things to a girl is great therapy for guys. If you find a guy who adamantly insists that guys and girls cannot be friends under any circumstances, be sure to thank him for his honesty, and then dump him off. No sense inviting trouble into your home.

The "damsel in distress" ploy: Does that old trick still work?

Sadly, yes. The color black will never go out of style. Black is an absolute. Women in distress (especially "reasonably attractive" ones) is another absolute. If a guy's hormones aren't enough to get him to come pester you, being in temporary need of a *hero du jour* is guaranteed to bring you men by the dozen.

By and large, men are so obsessed with trying to build themselves up so they can impress you that they will jump at any chance to be a hero of the moment. The hardest part of this ploy is not getting help when you want it, or just want some attention. It is deciphering the guy who is horny from the guy who is really a nice guy and just stopped to help. But as an excuse to get guys to give you attention, it works just as well as ever. If you do this, try different variations on the theme. Also, be certain to use this trick wherever there are wealthy guys who aren't too busy to stop and help you.

Final ~~thoughts~~ *ramblings*

And so we have finally come to the end of our merry little sojourn together. I hope you had fun reading this trite little text. I sincerely want everyone that reads this to smile, and I did what I could. I was homeless when I wrote this book (which is why it took me 12 years to finish it off). As it turns out, I was hungry, and I needed the money. Rather than hang around in front of 7-11 demanding change, I did my best and took a running stab at putting into words <u>what men secretly want girls to know</u>—*but we would obviously never tell you*—or admit to.

The whole point of writing this book was to inspire others not to let circumstance dictate their reality. **Don't wait** for the right situation to come along—start with what you have now and ignore anyone rude enough to try to convince you that you can't do anything you set your mind to. In these pages, you will find out what it takes to make men get all stupid over you, which is the only way that they will ever bother to listen to you, or do anything you want them to *on an ongoing basis*. <u>The moment we think we have you under control</u>, most of us are out the door, hanging out with our friends. Keep this book close to you at all times. **It works.** So much so that I suspect that more than a few guys will be upset at me for writing it, *not realizing that it really is for their own good.* C'est la vie . . . no? Bah! I just hope you liked it. I am off to other things. **I have twelve books to write to get the guys into shape.** Don't think for a moment that I am putting all of the work on you. Maybe someday we won't need books to learn how to <u>get along</u> and *treat each other well.* Until then, let's all keep reading.

"Mister X"
~~Dusty White~~

Appendix A

Fun Glossary of terms guys use, and terms that relate to guys

Bitches 'n Ho's:

A completely derogatory term that has been adopted by a vast cross-cultural mix of men under the age of 40 in the United States, used to classify all women (other than the guy's mother, and any other woman considered too old to have sex with) into two distinct camps:

"Bitches"—Women you marry (eventually). This is in contrast to "ho's"—unless the bitch cheats on you, in which case, *"the bitch is a ho!"* (it's all very scientific). Bitches only want one thing: what's in your wallet.

"Ho's"—Women (or girls) who are dumb enough, or have a low enough self-esteem to even have sex with "you" *(the guy who really has less going for himself than he likes to think).* Conversely, a "ho" can be a girl who has sex **with** (anyone or) **"everyone" BUT you,** in which case, *"the bitch is a ho."* Finally, "ho's" can be a generic term for women—meant playfully, but implying that sex is expected and deemed possible (so don't bother wearing any panties, and forget how to say "no").

Cars:

More than simple transportation. *City buses are transportation.* Cars are mobile expressions of one's personality, wealth, and level of refinement. Cars imbue status. Cars get you attention from women. Best of all, if you get bored, you can always jump in your car and drive someplace less boring, usually with friends (who are also bored).

Some guys like to work on cars; others like to race them. Still others like to "pimp them out" by adding all kinds of shiny gadgetry. A car is a possession you get to show off to the world as you pass by, to your friends, and of course, women. For many guys, their car,

SUV, bike (chopper or crotch rocket), is a natural extension of their penis. The more extravagant the ride, or the more he obsesses about how great his is, the more he is probably making up for something or other.

The moral of our story is: You can size a guy up extremely fast by what he drives, what he has done to it, how he treats it, and how much he needs to compare it to *other guys'* penises, I mean "cars" (sorry). The more obsessed he is with his penis, I mean "car" (*Dammit!* Sorry—again.), the easier it is to manipulate him, because he is obviously so insecure.

Chicks:

Casual generic term for women, or "girls" (usually meaning girls over the age of 17). Sounds infinitely better to men's ears than it ever will to a woman's. Contrary to popular belief among women, this term is not condescending. It is simply "masculine" slang.

Leather (or "Leathers"):

To most guys, the word leather in casual conversation means "my favorite old biker jacket I wear to look cool/sexy/tough . . ."

If a guy you are NOT married to lets you wear his leather *(assuming you are not stranded in a snowstorm),* he either bought it "broken in" from a store at the mall for a few hundred bucks *(cough-cough Poseur! cough-cough)* and, therefore, doesn't really care that much about it, or—and you will know if this is the case—he really likes you.

This is a few steps above letting you wear his letterman jacket in high school or college.

A real man will "occasionally" allow his very best friend(s) to borrow his favorite leather (or "sleeves" if the sleeves of said jacket are decorated with official H.A. flames—if you have to ask . . .), but letting a chick wear your sleeves or leather is not something you do unless she is naked (Yaaay!) AND freezing in a snowstorm. So if a guy lets you wear his sleeves, or his leather, and he is NOT a complete pussy, then this is a sign that he thinks of you as a very cool chick, which is good if you really like the guy.

170

Leather can also be a term for those in the SMBD scene (once again . . . if you need to ask—don't). Mention leather if you think the guy is kinky and see if he starts talking about jackets, or masks and ball gags. If he thinks you mean his sofa, just leave. There are plenty of "real men" out there.

Money:

A guy's secondary obsession (after "women"). "Money may not buy you love" (yes it does; don't kid yourself), but it buys all kinds of toys that attract women—and that makes (our) life definitely worth living.

The smartest among us (guys) make a certain amount and "bail out" of the rat race early, rather than perpetually chasing more, and more, in a vain attempt to reach some plateau that will not really make us any happier in the end.

Sports:

Timeless obsession of men worldwide. Sports help provide bonding experiences second only to war; opportunities to compete against other males (a favorite pastime), and the chance to show off to any females in the immediate vicinity. Be careful when discussing sports with strange men however: to some, the word implies actual physical activity (hiking, cycling, fencing, climbing, running, football, soccer, even a game of softball). We will call these men "athletes" or at least "active."

To an entirely different class of men (sometimes indistinguishable at first from "active" or "athletic" men), the word "sports" means only what is on TV—usually 6–8 hour marathons of sitting on a couch vigorously exercising one's vocal chords and hydrating with copious amounts of beer (after all shouting at the TV all day is hard work!).

Before settling for "just any man," ascertain his definition of the word "sports" by casually observing his weekend activities over a period of time.

Appendix B

List of MUST-OWN Guy Movies

If you are serious about having guys at your beck and call, there are movies you must see, *and then there are the movies you should own.*

In fact, <u>the difference between</u> *"Oh, I think I saw that"* and *"Oh, you mean (that movie)? Yeah, I have that on DVD. If you want to come watch it this weekend, just let me know."* <u>is often the dif-ference between</u> guys wanting to have sex with you—and guys fighting over you.

<u>Here are a list of movies you should own</u>:

Apocalypse Now: *(1979) Marlon Brando, Martin Sheen, Robert Duvall, Laurence Fishburne, Dennis Hopper, AND Harrison Ford. (Wow!) Directed by Francis Ford Coppola.*

This is an interesting study of masculinity. Marlon Brando is a bril-liant military mastermind. Send him out on a job, and leave him in the horrors of jungle warfare for too long, and he goes insane. But he is such a charismatic leader (and it helps that he always wins against the enemy) that his men swear absolute loyalty to him, because if anyone can get them home safely, someday—it his him.

Then you have the assassin, Martin Sheen. While he is on Brando's trail, you see the neutral masculine interaction of his escort. These guys don't know what Sheen's mission is, and it is not their job to care. They are just guys who signed up to defend our country and along the way ended up in the jungle on a boat.

Finally, there is Robert Duval. You just have to see the movie to understand how twisted of a genius *this* guy is, and why his men are so loyal to him. Martin Sheen runs into him along the way, and we get a rather one-sided account ("our" side) of what actual com-bat does to men. If you see war as a euphemism, this movie tells you a lot about guys in their daily lives.

<u>Memorable quote</u>: *"They were gonna make me a major for this, and I wasn't even in their fuckin' army anymore."*

NOTE: There are far more "memorable" quotes in this movie (*"Charlie don't surf!," ". . . smells like . . . victory,"* and so on), but that quote (above) reveals more about a man as an individual than any other single aspect of the movie. A good thing to know when you wonder why guys do the things they do.

The Big Lebowski: *(1998) Jeff Bridges, John Goodman, Flea (yeah—the guy from the Chili Peppers), Julianne Moore, Steve Buscemi, Philip Seymour Hoffman, Tara Reid. Directed by Joel Coen.*

"Dude."   Need I say more?

Guys love this film. If you can get through it, *and get it* (including the whole thing about the nihilists), then you probably understand what it is like to "be a guy," and should start teaching classes for women.

<u>Memorable quote</u>: *"Let me explain something to you. Um, I am not Mr. Lebowski. <u>You're</u> Mr. Lebowski. <u>I'm</u> the Dude. So that's what you call me. You know, that or, uh, His Dudeness, or uh, Duder, or El Duderino if you're not into the whole brevity thing."*

Blazing Saddles: *(1974) <u>Cleavon Little</u>, Gene Wilder, Slim Pickens, Harvey Korman, Madeline Kahn, Jack Starrett, Mel Brooks. <u>Written by the great Richard Pryor</u>, Mel Brooks, and other extremely talented writers. Directed by Mel Brooks.*

Blazing Saddles is the funniest movie ever made. End of story, show's over, *thank you and good night!* This is one the all-tme classic guy movies that some women just won't get. But that's okay, the very coolest women will. My girlfriend fell asleep during this movie. I dumped her.

<u>Memorable quote</u>: *"'Scuse me while I whip this out!"*

Caddyshack: *(1980) Rodney Dangerfield, Bill Murray, Chevy Chase, Ted Knight. Directed by Harold Ramis.*

A masterpiece of absurdist humor, along the lines of the immortal Mel Brooks and The Zucker Brothers. This movie is so stupid, and so raw, that you either roll on the floor hysterically (hint: alcohol helps) or you sit there stunned that anyone can possibly watch this trash.

There might actually be one guy under the age of 40 who falls into the latter category, but I highly doubt it. Pop this in for "the boys" (your favorite guy and his friends) and have a LOT of beer on hand. *Expect them to get rowdy and d-u-m-b.* If you can handle that, they will think of you as some kind of goddess. The biggest problem is that *their girlfriends* <u>will hate you</u> for being so fun and cool.

Also worth mentioning here: Rodney Dangerfield's **Back to School.** Not nearly as funny (no comedic supporting cast), but Rodney is hilarious in that.

<u>Memorable quote</u>: (Rodney Dangerfield, naturally)
"Hey everybody, we're all gonna get laid!"

Cool Hand Luke: *(1967) Paul Newman, George Kennedy, Strother Martin, Morgan Woodward, Dennis Hopper. Directed by Stuart Rosenberg.*

This movie is beautiful in an overtly masculine way. Stuart Rosenberg captured and displayed for us *the essence* of non-conformist struggle in an overly structured (and hardly "fair") world, the way Renoir snatched the essence of the moment from the very air around him, and masterfully cast it down onto canvas, where trapped, like a butterfly caught in a pool of amber, would be a thing of beauty we could witness forever. Entrancingly sad, this classic movie is a romance of the free spirit; our self-same butterfly, and the punishment for being an individual in a corporatized world.

<u>Memorable quotes</u>:

Boss Paul: "That ditch is Boss Kean's ditch. And I told him that dirt in it's your dirt. <u>What's your dirt doin' in his ditch?</u>"

Boss: "Sorry, Luke. I'm just doing my job. You gotta appreciate that."
Luke: "Nah—calling it your job don't make it right, Boss."

Luke: "Wish you'd stop bein' so good to me, Cap'n."

Captain: "What we've got here is . . . failure to communicate. S-Some men you just can't reach . . . So you get what we had here last week—which is the way he wants it . . . well, he <u>gets</u> it . . . I don't like it anymore than you men . . ."

Die Hard: *(1988) Bruce Willis, Reginald VelJohnson, Alan Rickman (yes . . . Professor Snape). Directed by John McTiernan.*

Forget Harry Potter! Alan Rickman is downright *evil* in this classic action movie. It's always better when you can really like/hate the bad guy in a movie. What makes this movie really great, however, is that this movie broke from the tradition of the overused Hollywood tripe: *Good Cop/Bad Cop; good cop goes bad, good cop's wife is kidnapped/killed and he has to go "bad" (blah, blah, blah).* Bruce Willis' character was the antithesis of action-movie hero at a time when Sylvester Stallone and Arnold Schwarzenegger were dominating the screens in over-the-top alpha-male belligerence.

Bruce Willis is just trying to go to his wife's company Christmas party. <u>This is right after she has dumped him for being a crappy husband.</u> He is pretty miserable throughout the film, in an "average guy trying to make it in the world while terrorists with machine guns are trying to run his day" kind of way. *And that is exactly why guys love it so much.* There is not a guy alive who doesn't sometimes feel like he is just going through his day while some terrorist (his boss, some governmental agency, his "ex") is trying to make his life miserable. All in all, a fun movie with a satisfying ending.

<u>Memorable quote</u>: *"Now I have a machine gun. Ho ho ho." (You really have to see the movie to get the sickness of this joke.)*

Dr. Strangelove or: How I Learned to Stop Worrying and Love the Bomb: *(1964) Peter Sellers, Peter Sellers, and Peter Sellers, George C. Scott, Slim Pickens, James Earl Jones. Directed by Stanley Kubrick.*

If you like black comedies, especially ones about the end of the world, and how impossibly screwed up our militaristic world view has become, this movie reigns supreme. This movie pairs up nicely with *Harold and Maude* for making the impossibly sad downright hilarious. But it is such a guy movie that much of the humor may not take. Enjoy it anyway.

<u>Memorable quote</u>: *"Mr. President, I'm not saying we wouldn't get our hair mussed. <u>But I do say no more than ten to twenty million killed, tops.</u> Uh, depending on the breaks."*

Fight Club: *(1999) Edward Norton, Brad Pitt, Helena Bonham Carter, Meat Loaf. Directed by David Fincher.*

This is a movie you really have to see at least 5 times, or not at all. It's that twisted. And it is definitely that important. If you have never seen the movie, you may think it is a move about fighting, or urban terrorism. But it is so much more than either of those. It is a movie about life—and what you do with it.

Memorable quotes:

"This is your life; and it's ending one minute at a time."

—and of course—

"No . . . I didn't quite catch that Lou."

The Godfather: *(1972) Marlon Brando, Al Pacino, James Caan, Robert Duvall, Diane Keaton, Abe Vigoda. Directed by Francis Ford Coppola, Novel by Mario Puzo.*

Arguably the best movie ever made (for guys), this is undoubtedly *the quintessential guy movie.* Sex*, violence, power. Mostly power. Too much to say here, other than you seriously need to own this movie. Pick a day and make it a "Godfather holiday" once a year and have guys over to watch it. They will think you can walk on water.

*There's no sex in this movie. This movie is so well made it doesn't need a cheap sex scene to get guys to watch it.

Memorable quote: *"I'm gonna make him an offer he can't refuse."*

The Godfather Part II: *(1974) Al Pacino, Robert Duvall, Diane Keaton, Robert De Niro. Directed by Francis Ford Coppola.*

Forget what I just said about *The Godfather* being the best movie of all time. THIS is the best movie of all time. Watch both movies. Take notes. Then argue with your favorite men which movie was better. This is the kind of argument you want to have. Be passionate. Have details. No matter who wins the argument, you win.

The fact that you can hold your own in a discussion on the merits of *The Godfather* versus *The Godfather Part II* will put you so far above other women (no matter how "hot") that they will need a telescope to see you. As to the alleged *The Godfather Part III*, you should know that the movie is despised by a good number of men. To others, this movie simply "does not exist." Decide for yourself.

Memorable quote: *"I don't want to kill everyone, Tom. Just my enemies."*

The Good, The Bad, and The Ugly: *(1966) Clint Eastwood, Lee Van Cleef, Eli Wallach. Directed by Sergio Leone.*

This is the classic "Spaghetti Western." This movie is so good that they should have moved Hollywood to Italy—even just for a year. Watch this a few hundred times, and you will understand men, and how they treat each other. Don't waste your time with imitations: ONLY WATCH The Director's cut.

NOTE—*Sometimes referred to as: Buono, il brutto, il cattivo, Il by American men who speak no Italian at all. IF YOU BUY THIS: Get "The Director's Cut." (Worth repeating.)*

Memorable quotes:

Tuco: *"God is on our side because he hates the Yanks."*
Man With No Name: *"God is not on our side because he hates idiots also."*

(also . . .)

Man With No Name: *"You see, in this world there's two kinds of people my friend: Those with loaded guns, and those who dig. You dig."*

The Lost Boys: *(1987) Kiefer Sutherland, Jason Patric, Corey Haim, Dianne Wiest, Barnard Hughes, Edward Herrmann, Corey Feldman, Jamison Newlander. Directed by Joel Schumacher.*

Part horror flick, part comedy, and all around guilty-pleasure pre-Seattle scene coolness, this is simply a fun movie. In fact, I would go as far as to say that it was The Warriors of the late '80s. Guaranteed a good night of camp and popcorn-consuming fun. Best in the background at a party, or snuggled up with your favorite guy. Then take him on a quick trip to Santa Cruz ("Santa Carla" in the movie) and see the boardwalk, the beach, and the bridge, if you can.

<u>Memorable quote</u>: *"One thing about living in Santa Carla I never could stomach . . . all the damned vampires."*

Raging Bull: *(1980) Robert De Niro, Joe Pesci. Directed by Martin Scorsese.*

Robert De Niro plays Jake LaMotta, a brutal boxer whose inner rage destroys everything worth living for in his life, and eventually himself. The guy is not very likeable, but the movie works due to the genius team that created it. Sometimes in life there are no heroes—and that is the beauty of this film.

A good movie to double up with this is:

On the Waterfront: *(1954) Marlon Brando, Karl Malden, Rod Steiger. Directed by Elia Kazan.*

This film defines the term *classic*. Low budget, shot on location (really seedy locations), harnessing some of the most talented actors of their day to rip the lid off of unionized corruption. *(Hey, look everyone! I'm a movie critic!)* This film is pretty brutal emotionally. Don't try to catch your guy crying during this movie. Just ignore it if he does. **8 Oscars;** *nominated for 12.* Do I really need to say anything more?

<u>Memorable quote</u>: *"You don't understand! I coulda had class. I coulda been a contender! I coulda been somebody, instead of a bum, which is what I am . . . Let's face it. It was you, Charley."*

(and that's where that line came from . . .)

The Road Warrior: *(1981) Mel Gibson. Directed by George Miller.*

The first of two sequels to *Mad Max,* this movie successfully established Mel Gibson as an action hero. You'll find lotsa "cars turned into assault vehicles" in this movie, which leads to lots of cool explosions. Creepy looking bad guys. All in all, a masterpiece of film designed to exploit the working-class male fantasy of rebuilding a car and saving the world from lunatic mutants in a post-apocalyptic world. *(See also: Mad Max.)*

Memorable quote: *"Greetings from The Humungus! The Lord Humungus! The Warrior of the Wasteland! The Ayatollah of Rock and Rolla!"*

Scarface: *(1983) Al Pacino, Steven Bauer, Michelle Pfeiffer. Written by Oliver Stone. Directed by Brian De Palma.*

Easily one of the best gangster films ever made, this movie cemented Al Pacino in American cinema history (like he wasn't already a shoo-in). The film is a remake of the 1932 Howard Hawks gangster classic, but it is impossibly rare for the remake to be *as good as the original.* Watch it with friends.

Memorable quote: *"Say hello to my little friend!"*
(Did you ever wonder where that line came from?)

The Terminator: *(1984) Arnold Schwarzenegger, Linda Hamilton. Directed by James Cameron.*

There were action movies before *The Terminator.* There were also a few cool Arnold movies before *The Terminator.* But this is the movie that made Arnold truly a household name. And he was the bad guy (which was really cool). This movie was so cool that it made "T2" (the sequel: *Terminator 2*) one of the most highly anticipated sequels ever.

Memorable quote: *"I'll be back."*
(Now you know who to blame.)

Also worth mentioning: *T2* (noted above), but forget *T3* altogether. It was a *huge disappointment,* after far too long of a wait. At this writing, it remains to be seen if the fourth movie of this franchise will be strong enough to hold up to the first two, and thus make the eventual boxed set worth buying.

NOTE: Some of the quotes (above) were verified though the Internet Movie Database (IMDB), *www.imdb.com.*

Here are a list of movies you should see:
(twice is better)

12 Angry Men (1957)
Animal House (1978)
Casablanca (1942)
Citizen Kane (1941)
Goodfellas (1990)
The Great Escape (1963)
The Lord of the Rings *(1, 2, and 3)*
The Maltese Falcon (1941)
The Manchurian Candidate (1962)
One Flew Over the Cuckoo's Nest (1975)
Pulp Fiction (1994)
Rear Window (1954)
The Seven Samurai (1954)
Slap Shot (1977)
Taxi Driver (1976)
The Warriors (1979)

Please note that the years in parentheses indicate the year the film was released. Rent THAT version, not the remake. This is especially true of *The Manchurian Candidate.*

Also recommended:

American Beauty (1999)
American History X (1998)
Chinatown (1974)
A Clockwork Orange (1971)
Das Boot *(The Boat; German)* (1981)
The Deer Hunter (1978)
The Dirty Dozen (1967)
Dirty Harry (1972)
Fast Times at Ridgemont High (1982)
The French Connection (1971)
Monty Python and the Holy Grail (1975)
Reservoir Dogs (1992) [exceptionally violent film]
The Silence of the Lambs (1991)

Appendix C

How I learned to stop worrying
and love women's magazines

I was feeling a bit randy the other day, and so I braved some of the women's magazines. Trust me, as guys we have all checked out the chicks on the covers to see if they are showing any cleavage.

Other than that, we may scan the cover if we are stuck behind some old lady with a hundred coupons at the grocery store—but ONLY if there are no Sports Illustrated or tabloid covers to stare at. Personally, I like the black and white magazine that usually prophesizes Elvis' return, or aliens abducting celebrities.

The only time we will actually read the cover of one of those magazines is if something catches our eye while we are looking for exposed breasts; something like "How to make your man forget his Ex" or some other nonsense like that. So don't expect us to know much about (let alone actually touch) any of your magazines. That said, I picked up a few and poked around, trying to tell them apart.

I don't remember much after that. Something about paramedics waving something that smelled really awful under my nose, and noticing how far up the ceiling looks in the supermarket when you are lying on the cold tile floor. I shook off my embarrassment at actually fainting in public like a little girl, and bought a case of beer to massage my bruised ego.

I thought about it a lot and decided I should call the editors of them and see what it is about these magazines that is so worth reading. On the following pages are the results of my survey:

Women's Magazines
I checked out

Cosmopolitan

This seems to be the granddaddy of all women's magazines, or grandmommy, or whatever . . . I think the copy I picked up weighed about a pound, which seemed quite a value for the price. If *SI* or *Playboy* had as many pictures of semi-naked women as this magazine seems to, we (guys) would never need to surf the internet—*ever.*

The editor I spoke to at *"Cosmo,"* as I have been told it is affectionately known as, was extremely polite—and downright helpful (I think she liked me—*that is hot*).

She was very understanding of my confusion at not seeing any footballs, computer sales, or stock market indexes in a magazine. She explained to me that *Cosmopolitan* is designed to be a girl's best friend ("just like diamonds"), and that every month they strive to help you find ways to get hot guys interested in you, have more fun in and out of relationships, and live a richer, fuller life—kinda like what I did in this book.

Wow, if I had *actually read Cosmopolitan,* maybe I would not have felt the need to write this book. Well, that was what I thought until the exquisitely nice editor informed me that, as a guy, if I *had* read an entire issue of *"Cosmo,"* cover–to–cover, my head would have exploded.

That would be <u>cool</u>*!*

Elle

Elle seems to be a French magazine at first, but it is printed in English. This confuses the mind. But when I called the home office *(in France no less!),* it turns out that they are a globally published magazine that focuses on beauty and style. I felt that we had struck a common bond, as *I myself* am focused on beauty and style.

I noticed that they had an astrology section. Being something of an astrology buff myself, I found this quite enjoyable. It seemed more skewed to a woman's point of view than I was used to seeing, but then I suppose that is part of the secret language you all speak to each other when we (guys) are not around. One day we will break open your secret codes and we will finally know your secrets. Until then, I think a nice yellow banana would be nice . . .

Seventeen

As a guy, I felt strangely drawn to this magazine, but upon picking it up, I felt *really creepy*, so I dropped it immediately, as if it was holy water and I was a vampire. I don't think adult men <u>should even know that this magazine exists</u>.

I would like to review it for you, *but it just seems wrong on every level*—so my advice is to check it out for yourself. I guess if you are seventeen, this is probably the magazine for you.

Appendix D

Recommended Reading

What follows are just a few books you might want to peruse if you are interested in getting the most out of guys, and **getting the most out of life** by having guys "help you out a bit" along on your way to personal happiness in life.

How to Win Friends and Influence People
By Dale Carnegie

What can I say? Do I really need to tell you that this is the most important book you will (probably never) read? You can find this book everywhere, at pretty much any price you like. In fact, you probably could not go through a day without meeting someone who owns (or did at one point) a copy of it. Buy the hardcover at a bookstore, buy a paperback on Amazon.com, get it at the library, or you can even find a copy at a garage sale or thrift sore. Excellent reading on any rainy day. The thing to know is that once you do read it—*and apply what you learned—you will be more popular than anyone you know.*

Well . . . that's about it. If I read any more books I think women would enjoy, I will be sure to let you know. I stopped by the library the other day and had a look around. It seemed like they had a *lot* of books there, no doubt on a *lot of subjects.*

Well, that's good . . . I suppose that keeps them in business. I got lost and ended up wandering out empty handed. (I had no idea where to start reading—with so many books to choose from—so I figured "why bother?") I guess I will have to stop back in some time.

Until then . . . I am off to catch the game on TV.

"Popozao!"

Help Pages

*Be sure to glance
through these*

Where to get help

I hope that none of you will ever need to use this section. On the following pages is a list of hotlines; most of which are available to you 24 hours a day. On the other end of the phone are trained, caring professionals. If you are in a bad situation, and need help leaving, *or you are not ready to make a decision and "just want to know what your options are," you can call and get answers to any questions you may have.*

You can usually call from any pay phone,
and most of the numbers are toll-free.

This section is organized by state. A full list of free resources is far beyond the scope of this book (my original attempt at this directory yielded over 300 pages, so I had to cut it down a bit). If you wish to find a more complete list of women's resources **listed by state and county,** please check the following websites or your local phone book. Most public libraries offer free internet access if you are unable to use a computer at home or work for whatever reason.

Websites that have a more thorough list of available resources:

www.aardvarc.org/dv/states/menu.shtml

For international listings and in-depth information, please visit:

www.safe4all.org/resource-list/

The National Domestic Violence Hotline # is

1-800-799-SAFE (7233)

The National Sexual Assault Hotline is 800-656-4673
Pop those numbers into your cell phone <u>now</u>

. . . and just in case you ever wondered . . .

The two national suicide hotline numbers are:

1-800-SUICIDE **(1-800-784-2433)**

for the National Hopeline Network, and

1-800-273-TALK **(1-800-273-8255)**

for the National Suicide Prevention Lifeline. Not that *you* will ever need them, but in case you ever want to call, you know *. . . There are good people on the other end of the line.*

Resources by state

(Please note that some of the toll-free numbers below ONLY work in that state.)

Alabama
Statewide resources
Alabama 24-hour Domestic Violence Hotline 800-650-6522
Alabama Coalition Against Domestic Violence 800-650-6522
Alabama Coalition Against Rape 334-264-0123
Child Abuse Reports 334-242-9500
Victim Rights Information 800-626-7676

Alaska
Statewide resources
Alaska Network on Domestic Violence and Sexual Assault 800-799-7233
Or call their non-toll free number: (907) 586-3650 **(also accepts collect calls)**
Alaska Office of Victim's Rights . . . . 907-272-2620 (or) 866-274-2620
Standing Together Against Rape (STAR) . . . 800-478-8999 (or) 907-276-7273

Arizona
Statewide resources
Arizona Coalition Against Domestic Violence 800-782-6400 (or) 602-279-2900
DV/Homelessness Shelter Hotline . . . . 800-799-7739 (or) 602-263-8900
Information and Referral Services Hotline *520-323-9373*
Community Information and Referrals: In the 520 area code . . . 800-352-3792
In the 602, 623, and 480 area codes 800-799-7739
Arizona Humane Society Project Safe House . . . . 602-997-7585 *Extension 134*
(Temporary foster care for pets of domestic violence victims. How cool is that?)

Arkansas
Statewide resources
Arkansas Coalition Against Domestic Violence 800-269-4668 (or) 501-907-5612
Arkansas Coalition Against Sexual Assault . . 866-632-2272 (or) 479-527-0900
Women and Children First *(Little Rock)* . . . . . 501-376-3219, or 800-332-4443
Saint Francis House Inc. *(Little Rock)* 501-664-5036
Provides casework and emergency food, clothing, medicine, rent and utility assistance to individuals in need.

California
Statewide resources
California Alliance Against Domestic Violence 800-524-4765
Battered Women's Support Services . . . . . . 877-520-5893 (or) 866-297-7443
Partnership to End Domestic Violence (www.cpedv.org) 800-524-4765
Free Battered Women . . . . 415-255-7036 extension 320
They help women who are in prison for defending themselves against DV.

Colorado

Statewide resources
Colorado Coalition Against DV . . . . 888-788-7091 (or) 303-831-9632
Colorado Coalition Against Sexual Assault . . 303-861-7033 (or) 877-372-2272
Gay-Lesbian-Bisexual-Trans. Anti-Violence . 888-557-4441 (or) 303-852-5094
Colorado Organization for Victim Assistance . 800-261-2682 (or) 303-861-1160

Connecticut

Statewide resources
Connecticut Coalition Against Domestic Violence 888-774-2900
24/7 Infoline: Referral, and Crisis Intervention Service 800-203-1234

Delaware

Statewide resources
Delaware Coalition Against Domestic Violence 302-658-2958
Domestic Violence Hotline (New Castle County) 302-762-6110
Domestic Violence Hotline (Northern Kent County) 302-678-3886
Domestic Violence Hotline (Kent & Sussex Counties) 302-422-8058
Latino/a Domestic Violence Hotline (Kent & Sussex Counties) . . 302-745-9874

Florida

Statewide resources
Florida Statewide 24-Hour Domestic Violence Hotline 800-500-1119
Florida Council Against Sexual Violence . . . . 888-956-7273 (or) 850-297-2000
Florida Abuse Hotline 800-962-2873

Georgia

Statewide resources
Georgia Coalition Against Domestic Violence 800-334-2836
Battered Women's Justice Project 800-903-0111
24-Hour Crisis Line 404-873-1766
Atlanta Gay Helpline 404-892-0661
Shelter Helpline 800-334-2836
Department of Corrections: Offender Status Hotline 888-656-7660
Georgia Crime Victim Compensation 404-657-1956

Guam

Statewide resources
Guam's 24 Hour Hotline 671-647-8833
Healing Hearts Rape Crisis Center 671-647-5351
Victim Advocates Reaching Out Hotline . . . . 671-477-5552 (or) 671-647-8833
Sanctuary **_Provides help_ at ANY TIME to youths 12 to 18** . . 671-475-7101
Sanctuary CAN ALSO provide emergency shelter if you need it.
Alee Shelter (_Women and Children Only_) 671-637-2533
Guma Sagrada (_Shelter for Disabled and Elderly_) 671-649-8881
Guma San Jose I & II (_For Individuals and Families_) 671-637-2957

Hawaii

Statewide resources
Hawaii State Coalition Against Domestic Violence 808-832-9316

Idaho

Statewide resources
Idaho Statewide 24-hour Domestic Violence Hotline 800-669-3176
Idaho Coalition Against Sexual And Domestic Violence 800-669-3176
WCA Women's Crisis Center 208-343-7025

Illinois

Statewide resources
Illinois Coalition Against Domestic Violence 217-789-2830
For a listing of LOCAL services, please see www.womenslaw.org/IL/IL_links.htm

Indiana

Statewide resources

Indiana Coalition Against Domestic Violence 800-332-7385
Statewide Domestic Violence Hotline 800-332-7385
Adult Protective Services 800-992-6978
Child Abuse Hotline 800-800-5556
Temporary Assistance for Needy Families 800-622-4932

Iowa

Statewide resources

Iowa Statewide Domestic Abuse Hotline 800-942-0333
Iowa Statewide Sexual Abuse Hotline 800-284-7821
Iowa Coalition Against Domestic Violence . . 800-942-0333 (or) 515-244-8028
Iowa Coalition Against Sexual Assault 515-244-7424
Department of Corrections Victim & Restorative Justice Programs 515-242-5742
Children & Families of Iowa 515-288-1981

Kansas

Statewide resources

Kansas Statewide Crisis Hotline *888-END-ABUSE* (888-363-2287)
Kansas Coalition Against Sexual and DV . . . 888-363-2287 (or) 785-232-9784

Kentucky

Statewide resources

Kentucky Domestic Violence Association 502-209-5382
Office of Child Abuse and Domestic Violence Services 502-564-9433
Kentucky Victim Notification Program (VINE) 800-511-1670

Louisiana

Statewide resources

Louisiana Statewide 24-Hour Domestic Violence Hotline 888-411-1333
Louisiana Foundation Against Sexual Assault 888-995-7273
Louisiana Coalition Against DV . . . . 888-411-1333 (or) 225-752-1296
Calcasieu Women's Shelter Hotline 800-223-8066
Rape Crisis Outreach 24-Hour Sexual Assault Hotline 337-494-RAPE (494-7273)
Or call their toll free number 888-255-RAPE (255-7273)

Maine

Statewide resources

Maine Coalition to End Domestic Violence 207-941-1194
For a listing of LOCAL services, see www.womenslaw.org/ME/ME_links.htm

Maryland

Statewide resources

Maryland Network Against DV*800-MD-HELP* (800-634-3577) (or) 301-352-4574
For a listing of LOCAL services, see www.womenslaw.org/MD/MD_links.htm

Massachusetts

Statewide resources

Jane Doe, Inc. Coalition Against Domestic Violence 877-785-2020
SafeLink Domestic Violence Hotline . . . . . . (English & Spanish) 877-785-2020
Network for Battered Lesbians & Bisexual Women Hotline 617-423-SAFE
Gay Men's Domestic Violence Project Hotline 800-832-1901
Massachusetts Victim Compensation & Assistance 617-727-2200
Massachusetts Office for Victim Assistance 617-727-5200
Department of Corrections Victim Services Unit 866-6-VICTIM

Michigan

Statewide resources

Michigan Coalition Against Sexual and DV . . 800-996-6228 (or) 517-347-7000
Michigan <u>Resource Center</u> Against Domestic & Sexual Violence . 517-347-7000
Michigan Victim Services 517-373-3740
Michigan Victims Alliance 517-487-8278

Minnesota

Statewide resources
Toll-free statewide crisis line 866-233-1111
Battered Women's Legal Advocacy Project, Inc. 800-313-2666
Minnesota Coalition For Battered Women . . . 651-646-6177 (or) 800-289-6177

Mississippi

Statewide resources
Mississippi Coalition Against DV . 800-898-3234 (or) after 5pm: 800-799-7233
Mississippi Adult Protective Services 800-222-8000

Missouri

Statewide resources
LEAD (services for hearing-impaired domestic violence victims) . *800-380-3323*
Missouri Coalition Against DV and Sexual Assault 573-634-4161
Missouri Victim Assistance Network 800-698-9199
Crime Victim Compensation 800-347-6881
Child Abuse and Neglect Hotline 800-392-3738
Department of Corrections: Victim Services 573-526-6516
Elder Abuse and Neglect 800-392-0210
Parental Stress Helpline 800-367-2543
US Attorney Advocate (Eastern) 314-539-6887
US Attorney Advocate (Western) 816-426-3122

Montana

Statewide resources
Montana Coalition Against Domestic Violence 888-404-7794 (or) 406-443-7794
Department of Corrections Victim Assistance 888-223-6332
Child Abuse and Neglect Hotline 866-820-5437
Elder Abuse Hotline 800-551-3191
Victim Notification (VINE) 800-456-3076
Victim Compensation 800-498-6455
Native Indian Crisis Association 406-338-7922
Seven Sisters Native Coalition (for Native American women) . . . 406-338-4881

Nebraska

Statewide resources
Domestic Violence Sexual Assault Coalition . 402-476-6256 (or) 800-876-6238
Nebraska Coalition for Victim Assistance 800-944-6282
Nebraska Crime Victims' Reparations Board 402-471-2828
Nebraska Child Abuse Hotline 800-652-1999
US District Attorney Victim Advocate 800-889-9124

Nevada

Statewide resources
Rape Crisis Center (Las Vegas) 702-366-1640
Rape Crisis Center (Mesquite) 800-752-4528
Rape Crisis Center (Laughlin) 800-553-7273
Nevada Domestic Violence Hotline 800-500-1556
Nevada Network Against Domestic Violence 775-828-1115
Child Abuse Reporting 800-992-5757
Child & Family Services 775-684-4400
Crime Victim Compensation (Reno/Northern) 775-688-2900
Crime Victim Compensation (Las Vegas/Southern) 702-486-2740

New Hampshire

Statewide resources
New Hampshire Coalition Against Domestic and Sexual Violence:
24-Hr Domestic Violence Hotline: 866-644-3574
24-Hr Sexual Assault Hotline: 800-277-5570
Statewide 24-Hour Hotline 800-RELAY-NH (800-735-2964)
New Hampshire Help Line 800-852-3388

(continued on next page)

Adult Protective Services 603-271-4680
Child Abuse Report Hotline 800-894-5533
Child & Family Services 603-444-0418
Legal Advice & Referral 800-639-5290
US Attorney's Office Victim/Witness Program 603-225-1552

New Jersey

Statewide resources
New Jersey Coalition for Battered Women *800-572-SAFE* (800-572-7233)
Statewide Domestic Violence Hotline *(Womanspace, Inc.)* 800-572-7233
Battered Lesbian Hotline (M-F 7:30p-9pm, Sat/Sun 12-2pm) . . 800-224-0211
Child Abuse Hotline *877-NJ-ABUSE* (877-652-2873)
New Jersey Crime Victim Compensation Agency 877-658-2221
Manavi for South Asian Women 732-435-1414
Office of Victim-Witness Advocacy 609-896-8855

New Mexico

Statewide resources
New Mexico Coalition Against DV . . . . 800-773-3645 (or) 505-246-9240
Domestic Violence Legal Resources Hotline:
(Albuquerque) 505-243-4300
(Statewide) 877-974-3400
Statewide Advocacy for Survivors of Abuse 505-982-2504
Child Abuse Reporting 800-797-3260
Department of Corrections Victim Services 877-842-8464
Lawyers Care Pro Bono Project 505-797-6000
Legal FACS 24 Hours Advocacy 505-217-0464
Morning Star House, Inc. 505-232-8299
New Mexico Victims' Rights Project 888-410-1084

New York

Statewide resources
NY State Adult DV Hotline . . *(Español) 800-942-6908* (English) 800-942-6906
NY City Domestic Violence Hotline (Bilingual) . *800-621-HOPE* (800-621-4673)
Senior Citizen Hotline 800-342-9871
Child Abuse Hotline 800-342-3720
Child Abuse and Neglect Prevention Information Line 800-342-7472
Office for the Prevention of DV . . . . 518-457-5800 (or) 518-486-6262
NY State Coalition Against Sexual Assault 518-482-4222
Crime Victim Compensation Board 800-247-8035
Crime Victims Helpline 800-771-7755

North Carolina

Statewide resources
North Carolina Coalition Against DV . . . . . . 888-232-9124 (or) 919-956-9124
North Carolina Crime Victim Compensation Services 800-826-6200
For a listing of LOCAL services, see www.womenslaw.org/NC/NC_links.htm

North Dakota

Statewide resources
ND Council On Abused Women's Services . . 800-255-6240 (or) 701-255-6240
Department of Corrections Victim Services 800-445-2322
For a listing of LOCAL services, see www.womenslaw.org/ND/ND_links.htm

Ohio

Statewide resources
Ohio Domestic Violence Network . . . . 800-934-9840 (or) 614-781-9651
Family Violence Prevention Center 614-466-0306
Center for Prevention of Domestic Violence . . . *216-391-HELP* (216-391-4357)
Ohio Coalition for Battered Women .888-622-9315
Attorney General Crime Victim Services 800-582-2877
Department of Corrections Victim Services *888-VICTIM-4* (888-842-8464)

(continued on next page)

Oklahoma

Statewide resources
Domestic Violence Intervention Services 24-Hour Crisis Line . . . 918-585-3143
SAFELINE 800-522-7233
Teenline *(teens can call for help, or someone to talk to)* 800-522-8336
Coalition Against DV and Sexual Assault . . .800-522-7233 (or) 405-524-0700
Child Abuse reporting 800-522-3511
Crime Victim Compensation 800-745-6098

Oregon

Statewide resources
Coalition Against Domestic & Sexual Violence 888-235-5333 (or) 503-230-1951
WomenSpace Domestic Violence Services . . 800-281-2800 (or) 541-485-6513
Crime Victim Outreach Coordinator 503-378-5348
US Attorney Victim Assistance 503-727-1036
FBI Victim-Witness Coordinator 503-224-4181

Pennsylvania

Statewide resources
Coalition Against Domestic Violence . . . . . . 800-932-4632 (or) 800-537-2238
Pennsylvania Coalition Against Rape *888-772-PCAR* (888-772-7227)
Office of the Victim Advocate: Probation and Parole 800-563-6399
Office of the Victim Advocate: Department of Corrections 800-322-4472
Pennsylvania Commission for Women 886-615-7477
Center for Lesbian and Gay Civil Rights *866-LGBT-LAW* (866-542-8529)

Rhode Island

Statewide resources
Coalition Against Domestic Violence . . . . . . 800-494-8100 (or) 401-467-9940
Attorney General: *Sexual Assault and Domestic Violence Unit* . . 401-274-4400
Rhode Island Legal Services 401-274-2652
Child Abuse Reporting *800-RI-CHILD* (800-742-4453)
Crime Victim Compensation Program 401-222-8590

South Carolina

Statewide resources
Coalition Against Domestic Violence and Sexual Assault 800-260-9293
State Office of Victim Assistance 800-220-5370
Crime Victim's Ombudsman 888-238-0697
Crime Victim's Legal Network 888-852-1900
Attorney General Victim Services 803-734-3740
Department of Corrections Victim Services 800-835-0304
Probation/Parole Victim Services *(fugitive hotline)* 888-761-6175
South Carolina Victim Assistance Network 803-750-1200

South Dakota

Statewide resources
South Dakota Domestic Abuse Hotline *800-430-SAFE* (800-430-7233)
SD Network Against Family Violence & Sexual Assault 800-670-3989
SD Coalition Against DV & Sexual Assault . 800-572-9196 (or) (605) 945-0869
South Dakota Suicide Hotline 800-691-4336
Missouri Shores DV Center Hotlines . . . . . . 800-696-7187 (or) 605-224-7187

South Dakota Children's Health Insurance Program **800-305-3064**

****CHIP provides health insurance coverage to uninsured children under age 19
whose family income is up to 200% of the federal poverty level.*** Wow!!*

(continued on next page)

Tennessee

Statewide resources
Coalition Against Domestic & Sexual Violence 800-289-9018 (or) 615-386-9406
Domestic Violence Coordinating Council 615-386-9406
Adult Protective Services 888-277-8366
Crime Victim Compensation Program 615-741-2734

Texas

Statewide resources
Texas Council On Family Violence 512-794-1133
Texas Department of Human Services: Abuse Hotline 800-252-5400
Texas Women's Advocacy Project:
General Legal Hotline *800-777-FAIR* (800-777-3247)
Family Violence Legal Line *800-374-HOPE* (800-374-4673)
Emergency Advocacy Hotline *888-325-SAFE* (888-325-7233)
Aid to Victims of Domestic Abuse:
Legal Services and Battering Intervention 713-224-9911
Battering Intervention 713-224-9911

Also:

Jane's Due Process . . . . . **24-hour Hotline:** *866-www-jane* (1-866-999-5263)
*Jane's Due Process provides emergency **help for teenagers** in need of choices.*

Utah

Statewide resources
Statewide 24/7 Toll-Free InfoLink *800-897-LINK* (800-897-5465)
Utah Attorney General 801-366-0260
After much searching, I could not find any resources that provided statewide emergency help in Utah, and I had to admit defeat. If you know of any, please contact me.

Vermont

Statewide resources
Vermont Network Against Domestic Violence and Sexual Assault:
Office line: 802-223-1302
Domestic Violence Hotline: 800-228-7395
Sexual Assault Hotline: 800-489-7273
Adult Protective Services 800-564-1612
Advocacy for Immigrant Women 802-479-7547
Vermont Center for Crime: Victim Services 800-750-1213

Virginia

Statewide resources
Virginia Family Violence & Sexual Assault 24-Hour Hotline 800-838-8238
Department of Corrections: Victim Services 800-560-4292
Department of Criminal Justice: Victim Services 804-786-4000
Attorney General Victim Notification 800-370-0459
Virginia Crime Victim Assistance Line 888-887-3418

Washington

Statewide resources
Statewide 24-Hour Domestic Violence Hotline 800-562-6025
Family/Friends of Violent Crime 800-346-7555
Office of Crime Victim Advocacy 800-822-1067
Department of Social Services Victim Services 360-902-7602

West Virginia

Statewide resources
Call the national DV number or 9-1-1 . . . . (sorry)
Division of Corrections: Victim Assistance 304-558-2036

After much searching, I could not find any resources that provided statewide emergency help in West Virginia. I am deeply disappointed. If you know of any, please contact me directly. (me@dustywhite.net)

Wisconsin

Statewide resources

Call the national DV number or 9-1-1 . . . .(sorry again)
UNIDOS (Latina victims of domestic violence) 800-451-6095
Crime Victim Compensation Program 800-446-6564
American Indians Against Abuse 715-634-9980

After much searching, I could not find any resources that provided statewide emergency help in Wisconsin. I am deeply disappointed. If you know of any, please contact me.

Wyoming

Statewide resources

Coalition Against DV & Sexual Assault *Crisis Line:* **800-990-3877**
Wyoming Crime Victims Center 888-707-8979
Attorney General: Victim Services 307-777-7200
Their toll-free hotline (for victims only) is *888-996-8816*

Other important phone numbers
I hope you never need:

Ewwww!! You swallowed what?!!

Poison Help hotline 800-222-1222

• 24 hours a day • 7 days a week • free of charge

. . . and just in case you missed it earlier:

The National <u>Domestic</u> <u>Violence</u> <u>Hotline</u> # is

1-800-799-SAFE (7233)

The National <u>Sexual</u> <u>Assault</u> <u>Hotline</u> is

800-656-4673

1-800-SUICIDE (800-784-2433) for the National Hopeline Network, and *1-800-273-TALK* (800-273-8255) is the National Suicide Prevention Lifeline. (Yeah, yeah, I'm back on *that* again.)

1-800-ALCOHOL

This is a <u>nationwide help and referral</u> hotline for alcohol and drug problems. The phones are answered by individuals trained to assist callers 24 hours a day, 7 days a week.

Free information from the
Centers for Disease Control and Prevention
(formerly the CDC)

800-CDC-INFO (or) **800-232-4636** *(or) 888-232-6348 TTY*
(or) 404-498-1515 (or) 800-311-3435

Got a question for the CDCP?
*(Like when are they going
to get around to CURING cancer?*)*

You can call these guys 24/7 (at the CDC) and get free, anonymous, confidential HIV/AIDS information in English *and* Spanish
(it's a great way to practice your español). **AND you can also get
referrals** to appropriate services, *including clinics, hospitals, local
hotlines, counseling and testing sites,* legal services, health depart-
ments, support groups, educational organizations, and service
agencies throughout the United States. If you even think you might
need help—this is the place to call! Or go to: ***www.cdc.gov***

*(*Please do __not__ call the CDC and ask them when they are going to cure Cancer
once and for all. They are working on it even as we speak.)*

Gay and Lesbian National Hotline
888-THE-GLNH (or) 888-843-4564
M-F 4pm-12am, Sat 12pm-5pm Eastern Time

They provide *free and confidential telephone peer-counseling and
local resource information* for gay, lesbian, bisexual, transgender
and questioning people of all ages. If you have questions, they are
here to answer them.

National AIDS Hotline
1-800-342-AIDS

24-hour hotline provides information, education, and answers
questions regarding AIDS, testing facilities, and medications used
for treatment. Anonymous—*free*—informative. So what are you
waiting for? Call them!

196

National Herpes Hotline
919-361-8488 M-F 9am-6pm (Eastern Time)

Trained Health Communication Specialists are available to address questions related to transmission, prevention, and treatment of herpes simplex virus (HSV) *and* the hotline <u>also provides support for emotional issues</u> surrounding herpes *such as self-esteem and partner communication.* I wish we had more of *that kind* of support in society, generally speaking.

National STD Hotline
1-800-227-8922 (or) 800-342-2437 (or) 800-344-7432 (Español)

<u>Provides useful information</u> on sexually transmitted diseases (STDs), such as chlamydia, gonorrhea, HPV/genital warts, herpes, and HIV/AIDS, and referrals to local clinics.

Victims of Crime Help Line
800-FYI-CALL (or) 800-394-2255

Through its national database, the National Center for Victims of Crime refers callers to an array of critical services including crisis intervention, research information, assistance with the criminal justice process, counseling and support groups.

This last set of numbers is of special significance. It deals with the exploitation and abuse of children. *If you even suspect abuse,* it is your duty to make a call, and <u>let the professionals sort things out</u>. If you know of a child who is being abused *and you have exhausted all other resources* and you still can't get any help, I want you to call me, and I will personally come kick the ass of anyone who beats a child.

National Center for Missing and Exploited Children
800-THE-LOST (or) 800-843-5678

<u>This is the number to call</u>. *Call this number immediately* if you think you have spotted a child who is missing.

(continued on next page)

Childhelp USA
800-4-A-CHILD (or) 800-422-4453

The Childhelp National Child Abuse Hotline is available 24 hours a day, 7 days a week. If you need help or have questions about child abuse, call the Childhelp National Child Abuse Hotline <u>and then push 1 to talk to a counselor</u>.

The Hotline counselors are there 365 days a year to help kids, and adults who are worried about kids they suspect are being abused. You can call this number if you live in the United States, Canada, Puerto Rico, Guam, or the U.S. Virgin Islands. **The call is free and anonymous.** (The Hotline counselors don't know who you are and you don't have to tell them.) There won't be a charge for the call on your telephone bill if you use a regular phone or a pay phone. *If you use a cell phone, there may be a charge and it may show up on the telephone bill.* <u>Don't use a cell phone if you want to be sure your call is a secret</u>.

CyberTipline
800-843-5678

The CyberTipline handles leads from individuals *reporting the sexual exploitation of children.* <u>Please call if you have information</u> of ANY child being sexually exploited. Your information will be forwarded to law enforcement for investigation and review, and, when appropriate, to the Internet Service Provider.

About the author

Dusty White is a humble arms dealer in the endless battle of the sexes. He is a former professional psychic and astrologer with an international clientele of over ten thousand. Dusty retired from one-on-one counseling to begin his writing career in 1994 with a dating advice book for men entitled *How to be a Sexual God (in three easy lessons!)*. He is currently working on his ninth book, *Aphrodite's Book of Secrets*.

Passionately devoted to the fight against breast cancer, Dusty donates a large portion of his book royalties directly to The Avon Foundation and Breast Cancer Crusade, volunteers, and is a crew member for their annual walk. He is also the founder of *www.realmenwearpink.org*—a non-profit site designed to educate and enlighten men on the need to stop ignoring the issue and start helping find a cure.

"No, Mister Bond. I expect you to be helpless before the army of women who have read my book."

About the artist

Katrina Joyner was a fairy princess once, but then she woke up and discovered the power of the pen. After graduating with her BA in anthropology, her true purpose revealed itself as a comic book artist and all-purpose megalomaniac. Between plotting global destruction and discovering lost metropolii, she spends her days and nights drawing pictures and being assuaged by cats.

She has been the co-owner of Pentagram Komix and Graphix with which she edited and illustrated *Kinships* magazine, wrote and illustrated *Sidhe in Shadow, a Little Book of Seven*, and produced *Avenia*. Recently, *Battle of Angels* was published in two consecutive issues of *Moshi Moshi*. She has also been seen in galleries and found herself approached by collectors for her angels, fairies, and mermaids. In her super rare spare time, she creates *Akashik, the Battle of Angels* which is the sequel to her first Angelic endeavor. Her main website is *www.akashikonline.com*.

1620869

Made in the USA